HOW TO WIN WITH YOUR DATA VISUALIZATIONS

THE 5 PART GUIDE FOR JUNIOR ANALYSTS TO CREATE EFFECTIVE DATA VISUALIZATIONS AND ENGAGING DATA STORIES

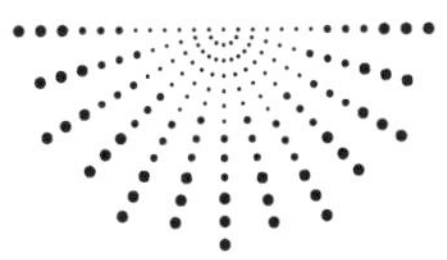

ELIZABETH CLARKE

TABLE OF CONTENTS

A Free Gift From Me to You!

The Winning Data Visualization Checklist

Good Average Poor

Make sure every visualization you create has all the elements that lead to a successful presentation!

Scan the QR code or visit ElizabethSClarke.com to get yours Free!

Download Here!

INTRODUCTION

"Data are just summaries of thousands of stories – tell a few of those stories to help make the data meaningful."

— CHIP AND DAN HEATH, NEW YORK TIMES BESTSELLING AUTHORS.

Data volume reached 79 zettabytes (ZB) by the end of 2021. By the end of 2025, that figure is expected to more than double to 181 ZB. To be clear, 1 ZB is 1 billion terabytes!

FIGURE 0.1

As impressive as those numbers are, none of those bytes would amount to much if they were not translated into an easily digestible format.

Enter left stage... More specifically, data storytelling.

For decades, the traditional way of presenting data was to pull out the old faithful pie or bar chart and spit out facts like a robot reciting the numbers on a spreadsheet. In such scenarios, most often, the listeners needed clothes pins to keep their eyes open. There was often the request to have the same information sent over through email or another method for "review" - a cleverly disguised way of gaining the information that was not digested during the boring presentation.

Ensure that is not the reality that you face when presenting data by tossing tradition out the window. Basic charts and numbers just do not cut it anymore. When most people have the attention span of a squirrel hopped up on caffeine, there needs to be a more compelling, more enticing way of delivering this data. And this is what data storytelling is all about – remixing the quantitative and qualitative nature of data and bringing the point across in a way that makes other people want to listen and learn more.

Over the last few years, the data industry has exploded in growth because this secret is out of the bag. Politicians use data storytelling to persuade voters to place the tick on their side of the ballot with touching commercials highlighting their contributions to the community. Marketing departments use it so that their brands touch your heart, and thus, you fork over some of your hard-earned cash before you make a conscious decision to do so. Data storytelling drives innovation and product development and adds to the zeros on the bottom line of major corporations like Coca-Cola, Mercedes Benz, and Amazon.

The examples of effective data storytelling in action are almost endless because it has been realized that there needs to be a change in the way we present data to conferences, seminars, potential and existing clients, customers, business executives, and more.

Through this change, others can happen. Without this change, most of these many bytes of information would go unnoticed.

This change does not have to just happen on a big business level.

This change can start with you.

As an established marketer with a repertoire of scaled brands, I have met many people in my line of work. I have met people new to the industry who want to leave a mark when making their first few presentations. I have met people who have made presentations in the past but failed to drive the message home to their bosses, board members, and other listeners. I have met small business owners who are stumped about how to win over new clients and customers when telling their brand stories. I have met people who simply want to have the know-how of crafting a captivating and engaging presentation in their back pocket so that they can pull it out whenever they need it.

All these people had one thing in common even though they came from a vast array of industries – They were struggling to present data in an effective, straightforward way that gets to the heart of the message they were trying to convey. These people had figured out that pulling out the old presentation board and pointing at charts and numbers does not make an impact and were seeking a better way.

If you can relate to how these people feel, this book was created specifically to help you get ahead of the curve and discover how to develop storytelling expertise that will give your presentations the panache they need to hit hard and hit home.

Data storytelling and visualization are quite hefty words for the tongue to lift, but they are not as complicated as they sound. They do not always have to involve learning to code or sweating over complex charts, as many assume. They are simply methods of clearing the clutter that zettabytes of data can produce to reveal a clean, concise goal around which a story can be created to drive change. This book helps you clear the clutter and create that path with ease.

You, too, can impress your boss and other executives with your presentation and data visualization skills. You can also win over new clients and customers and convince the existing ones to recommend you to their peers. You can convert data to dollar signs for your company and be on the fast track to your next promotion. The things that you can do by supporting data with a story are only limited by your imagination. You have the power to drive change and be part of this evolution of how data is presented and consumed.

You can do all of this and more by learning the five parts of crafting an effective and engaging data story. This book was broken down into five parts to make it easy for you to understand the strategies and knowledge outlined in the pages to come. You'll also have a guideline to follow when creating visuals and presentations. Let me give you a brief breakdown so that you get the gist of the exciting things to come:

THE FOUNDATION, THE NARRATIVE

You need to be able to quiet the noise of all the bytes of data and focus on what is truly important – the goal of your presentation. The goal is what allows for the proper development of the narrative of your data story. Your narrative defines the sequences of events and how you will layer your data for the best appeal. The narrative structures the whole story and holds everything together. Call it your data story glue, if you will. Without this glue, everything will inevitably fall apart. Without a solid narrative, not even the best visuals will salvage the wreck that the presentation is bound to be.

This part of the book focuses on helping you drill down on your presentation goal and how to sequence your data story around it for an easy, natural flow that resonates with your audience and solves the right solution.

CAPTIVATING YOUR AUDIENCE

A good data story is effective not just because of what you say but *how* you say it. To deliver your message most effectively, you need to understand your audience and speak their language. Captivating your audience with an engaging story is what plants the seed to significant change and growth.

CHOOSING THE RIGHT CHART

Now, do not get me wrong. I am not knocking the tremendous contribution that a good chart or well-dressed set of numbers can have to a presentation. The problem is that too many people focus solely on this and forget the narrative to support these data visualizations.

The correct chart presented at the right time can take a simple analysis and give it a visual form that people can use to develop a mental image of what you are presenting. This will help your presentation stick in their minds. It will make *you* memorable.

Data visualization is another crucial component of the data storytelling process that you must nail on the head. You will surely learn all you need to know about presenting effective data visualizations in this part of the book.

A WINNING DESIGN

Sight is the most used of all the human senses. Use that knowledge to your benefit. Do not just drop bland, tasteless charts and graphs on your audience's laps and call it a day. That will only leave a bad taste in their mouths and make you look less than the competent business person you are.

The face of any data visualization is the design. Having clean, concise, clutter-free designs is crucial to keeping your audience informed *and* engaged. As they say – presentation is everything. When it comes to data storytelling, you need to take the saying literally and figuratively.

CRAFTING A WINNING DATA STORY

The parts discussed above are essential, but none of them will give your presentation the edge it needs alone. You have to bring them all together to amaze, astound, educate, and convince your audience. This last part of the book shows you how to do just that, painlessly and cohesively.

I run into large amounts of data every day during my career in product marketing and social analytics. If you are anything like me, you find yourself fascinated with the components that make up company growth statistics, consumer and social analytics, sales figures, expenditure reports, and all the other numbers that show a company's performance. While these figures excite the senses of the data science nerd in me, I also realized that they could look like a foreign language to someone else. I have a few failed presentation stories of my own that I can tell.

When I was new to my career, I struggled to translate these figures. I would present basic, uninspiring charts with little information—stuttering at even the simplest questions. I always knew there had to be a more effective way to present data. Many failed presentations have taught me the best ways to transform any form of data into a language that everyone can understand. Translation through storytelling is a method that cannot be beaten.

Data storytelling is a vital part of any company's growth and management. Big businesses need it and so do small ones. Executives that have proved their mettle need it no matter how much they advance in their careers, and so too does the intern just starting in a field. My passion is to help as many people and businesses across the board take raw data and translate those bytes into stories that encourage change that allows meeting goals and targets. Call me quirky, but I always love when people reach out to me with stories about how the words I have written have helped inspire the change they need to take their professional lives to the next level.

I hope to hear a similar story from you. A data story of how much you have achieved using the words in this book, perhaps.

I suggest you get out a highlighter and mark anything you find valuable and worthy of remembering. One of my favourite tricks for revisiting valuable information with ease.

The data shows that anyone who reads past this page to the first chapter dramatically increases their chances of becoming a data storytelling superstar. So, what are you waiting for? Turn the page!

1
THE FOUNDATION OF DATA STORYTELLING - DEVELOPING THE NARRATIVE

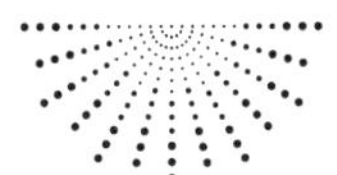

"The goal is to turn data into information and information into insight."

— *CARLY FIORINA, FORMER CEO, HEWLETT PACKARD*

With the many, many bytes of information available for relating to other people, how do you decide which ones deserve precedence and should be added to your slides? That is a fundamental question when approaching data storytelling. If this question has come to your mind, you have set yourself up with the right mindset to present data in the most digestible way to your audience.

The answer of which bytes of information you will relate to your audience depends on your final goal in the presentation. Too many business professionals get stuck on the visual aspects of the presentation and leave the information that needs to be relayed as an afterthought. But it is truly the other way around. The visuals do not matter if your audience cannot follow a defined path from the initial insight to a solution.

A narrative is about developing a language that allows for augmenting data in the most effective way to deliver to an audience so that the people in the audience are not left confused and trying to piece together these bytes of information. The narrative is the vehicle that conveys insights on the data that has been collected to the audience.

There are 3 main components of a great narrative. The *what,* The *who*, and the *how.*

The *What:* *What* is the goal of your presentation? What insights do you need to convey? What solutions do you need to guide your audience toward? *The "what"* is arguably the most important part of any data story. Without having a goal in mind, you will not know what insights to bring forward and how you will effectively present them.

The *Who:* Who are you presenting to? Knowing this is essential when presenting data because you need to know what they already know, and what they don't. What you present to your product manager vs. the CEO is very different. Finding out *who* you're presenting to will allow you to determine what you need to present and how you will present it. This will be covered more in-depth in chapter 2.

The *How:* Now that you know what you're presenting and who you're presenting it to, how you will do it should come naturally. Based on what you've already learned, you can select specific insights with supporting information and transmit them through beautifully crafted data visualizations in a favorable sequence. Of course, the bulk of the book shows you exactly how to do this, so I will not go any more in-depth here. Keep reading!

STRUCTURE

How will you structure all this information and present it effectively?

When relaying information, an effective structure I like to follow is the hook, the aha moment, and the solution.

The hook comes at the beginning of your data story. It is what captures the attention of your audience. The hook can be a question or stating a problem that this audience shares as a commonality, supported with a simple insight. It gets the audience thinking and engaged.

The "aha" moment is your audience coming to a favorable conclusion on their own, based on your strategic delivery of insights. Simply telling someone what they should do rarely works. Strategically delivering information so that your solution seems like the only option is crucial for a successful data story. (Of course, this is only if you've done the proper analysis and believe it is the right course of action. Ensure you don't leave any crucial data out. In more complex situations, having multiple solutions can also work in your favor, so your company comes to the best conclusion possible.)

The solution, is the reiteration of your end goal and call to action. This is where valuable business change happens. Getting your audience to come to this conclusion on their own and simply reiterating it to validate their realization is the best-case scenario.

Understanding the hook, aha moment, and solution gives you a great structure to base your narrative off. What information should be delivered as the hook, what will be the central insight of the presentation, and what is the goal of it all.

Let's run through an example.

Your company's primary goal is to gain new customers for maximum growth. However, your analysis leads to discovering there are few returning customers, leading to losses over time. You've discovered not enough attention has been targeted toward giving new customers an incentive to come back a second time and become recurring customers.

Simply stating this might not be enough. The audience of executives might just see consistent customer growth and want to stick with the strategy. However, constantly acquiring new customers means a lot is spent on advertising. We need to change our focus and build a robust and reliable customer base instead of a large volume of customers. How would you hook this to the reader? What are some possible solutions to the problem? How can you layout the information gradually, so the audience concludes on their own? In this case, a straightforward narrative could be:

Hook:

"It is extremely costly to acquire new customers at the rate we do so, and it is not a sustainable strategy. Our advertising costs are growing faster than our profits." (Show them that something has to change without relaying the details)

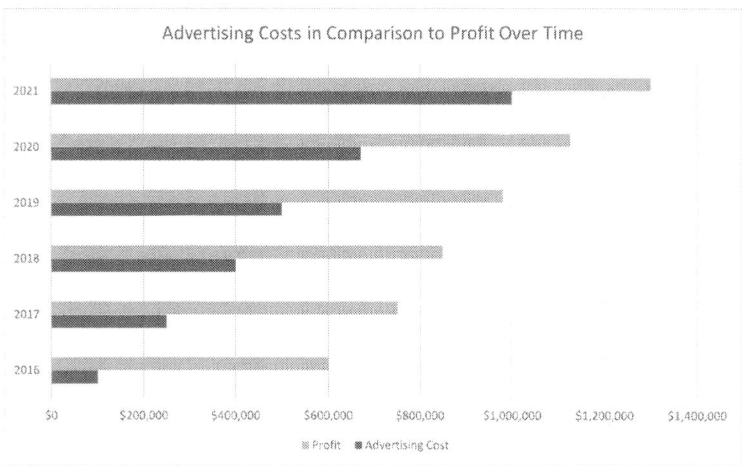

FIGURE 0.2 Horizontal bar graph comparing advertising costs to profits from 2016-2021.

Aha moment:

"While our focus is on acquiring new customers, few become consistent or even return. Our initial growth strategy was effective, but it is now becoming an issue in the business's long-term growth. We are spending a dollar to get a dime, over and over. As you can see, only 7% of our customers are returning customers, yet they make up 38% of the revenue. "(They realize what they are doing isn't sustainable, and they should be focusing on keeping customers, not just acquiring new ones)

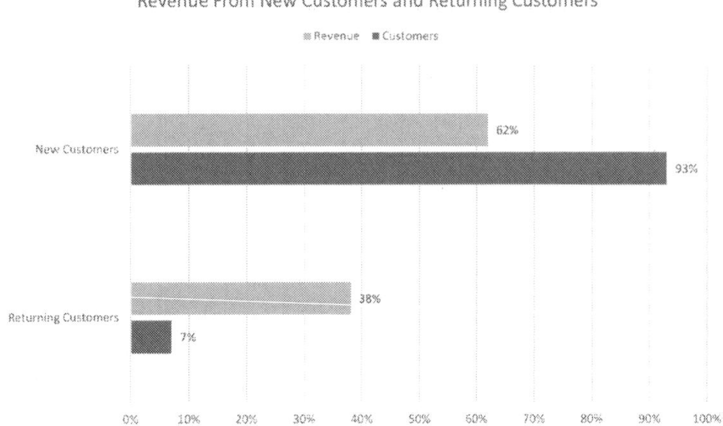

FIGURE 0.3 Comparing revenue of returning customers vs one time customers.

Solution:

"We can create long-term success and a better customer base by incentivizing customers to return. Allocating more budget to retargeting campaigns can also create many loyal customers." (A good solution is one that an audience comes to independently. Your main points should guide them where they need to go. In some cases, the solution is a reiteration of what they concluded on their own)

TYPES OF DATA

When compiling a presentation, an important thing to note is what you need to showcase. The type of data you're presenting determines the visualizations you use and the timeline in which you present it. Let's look at some common data types.

Trends

Presenting trends focuses on how figures rise and fall over a given amount of time and how these patterns of number behavior affect the audience. For example, a business analyst may present data to the executives that show sales figures rise towards the end and beginning of the year but dip around the middle of the year. Using this data, the narrative can be focused on why these figures are so and what can be done to increase sales when there is traditionally a decrease.

FIGURE 0.4 Scatter plot showcasing data trend throughout the year.

Comparisons

Showcasing comparisons builds on trends and shows how data changes over time in relation to specific periods. For example, let's say the revenue from a product launched in 2017 was on a steady incline until 2020, where it started to trend downward. We can look at other metrics from 2017 and 2020 to see if any significant changes in our business strategy or our market could've caused this. Catching a potential downward trend early on is critical for correcting it. We can also compare it to the performance of other products.

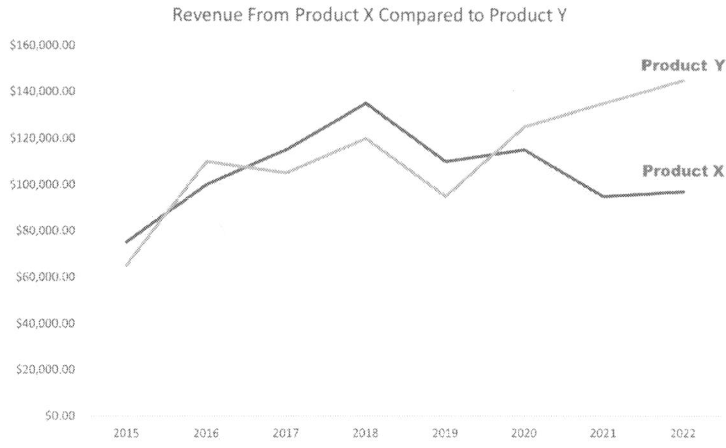

FIGURE 0.5 Comparison of two products of time

Rank Order

Communicating a hierarchy of factors to make a large amount of detail easier for the audience to digest. For example, the business analyst may present a table highlighting the best performing and worst performing campaigns. With this data, the executives can reallocate the budget and focus on their top converting revenue streams. Also, the marketing team can focus on promotions that showcase their best-selling softwares.

	Q1	Q2	Q3	Q4
Campaign 1	$50,000	$85,000	$75,000	$98,000
Campaign 2	$75,000	$79,000	$65,000	$86,000
Campaign 3	$100,000	$110,000	$90,000	$125,000
Campaign4	$56,000	$59,000	$50,000	$67,000
Campaign 5	$43,000	$69,000	$60,000	$65,000
Campaign 6	$78,000	$70,000	$77,000	$82,000
Campaign 7	$68,000	$67,000	$60,000	$77,000
Campaign 8	$55,000	$50,000	$56,000	$62,000

FIGURE 0.6 Table highlighting campaign performance.

Statistical Relationships

Statistical relationships allow the audience to know the relationship between different data types and how a change in one variable will cause an increase in the other. As an example, a business could be monitoring website traffic throughout the day to find the busiest times.

FIGURE 0.7 Line graph showcasing website visitors over a 12 hour period.

"***Quick tip*** *- A Quarter is a three-month period on a company's fiscal year that acts as a basis for periodic financial reports and the paying of dividends. A quarter refers to one-fourth of a year and is referred to as Q1 (January, February, March) Q2 (April, May June) Q3 (July, August, September), and Q4 (October, November, December). You will be seeing these terms used throughout the book.*"

Counterintuitive Data

This narrative shows surprising data that contradicts what the norm is. The counterintuitive nature of data invites further exploration, especially in instances where it has an adverse or alternatively, favorable impact on the business. Perhaps you have a spike in sales in January and July, which are normally two of the slower months. This unexpected data needs further exploration as to why this happened to determine if more sales can be derived from the revealed answer.

FIGURE 0.8

IMPORTANT THINGS TO CONSIDER

A good narrative gives you direction and purpose. It is essential for giving meaning to random bytes of information. Some baseline knowledge to have when presenting data are:

Only Present Relevant Data:

For example, let's say we're using our example from before, comparing new customers to recurring customers. It would be beneficial to compare sales between new customers and returning customers over the last year or more, but presenting these figures on a month-by-month basis doesn't tell the audience enough and is irrelevant based on this situation.

However, you cannot throw all of this data at your audience, expecting them to understand it even if you do. This will only serve to make your audience feel like a leaf in a thunderstorm - with no sense of direction of which byte of data to grasp first.

Cite only Credible Data

From the tons of available data, you need to remember that not all data sources are relevant or credible when presenting your data story. Understanding this allows you to specify what types of data you will present and where you cite this data.

Your audience needs to trust that the information you are sharing with them is credible. It needs to ensure people look at you as a credible source of information, and when they relay that information forward, it is accurate.

All the data that you need while creating your presentation might not be available immediately. Because the narrative of your data story helps guide the purpose of your presentation, you can then reason what information should be included in your presentation and approach the suitable sources for that missing data.

Develops A Clear Path

Building your narrative beforehand is essential for your presentation to be effective. It allows you to format the correct information in the appropriate sequence to lead your audience to the desired outcome, avoiding mid-presentation fumbles and confusion.

This is because a narrative helps define the events that must be touched on to reach your goal. Those events can then be broken down into plain language for a straightforward presentation. Like all good stories, the narrative must have a beginning, a middle, and an end.

Development of Proper Visualizations to Best Match the Context

Graphs, charts, photos, text, maps, tables. All of these charts and more can be used to create an effective and engaging presentation. However, just because they can be used doesn't mean you should use them.

Building a narrative allows you to select the proper chart for the data and any extra visuals required by your audience. If you were presenting last quarter's numbers to the project manager, you could keep it simple and straight to the point, as they are familiar with the campaign and its details. However, if you have to showcase this quarter's figures at an executive level, they might need more insight. Potentially a comparison between quarters throughout the year and some projections for the new year. We will dive deeper into presenting to your audience in chapter 2.

Using visuals that are not effective for your data story can confuse your audience far more than enlightening them. Therefore, it is imperative that you choose the proper visualization to enhance your details. We will go deeper into selecting and designing visualizations in chapters 3 and 4.

DEVELOPING THE NARRATIVE OF YOUR DATA STORY

Step 1 - Identify the Goal of your Data Story

To set up the goal for your data story and subsequently, set up the foundation for the narrative, there are a few questions that you need to ask yourself before you do anything else. These questions include:

- What is the problem that will be presented in your data story?
- What is the possible solution or solutions for solving that problem?

- What would you like to achieve by the end of your data story?
- What call-to-action can you strategically place in your presentation that will likely cause your audience to react in the way you would like?
- What takeaways would you like your audience to live with by the end of your data story?

Answering these questions thoroughly will allow you to set up the plot for your data story. You will know the beginning, middle, and end of that story so that you can extract data in alignment with that vision.

The important thing to remember when answering these questions is to let the data guide the narrative. Sometimes we believe that data is driving us in a particular direction, but picking out only irrelevant information will misguide us. To make sure you have the correct data and it is guiding you in the proper direction involves doing a few activities. Such activities include:

- Making comparisons of different sets of data. This will allow you to form correlations to see how these datasets relate to each other.
- Look for trends. Trends allow you to note how different aspects of the business are developing, changing, or remaining stagnant.
- Noting anomalies. Anomalies are sets of data that do not align with what you expect or are outside the norm. Noting anomalies will prompt you to look at *why* this is happening and whether this is in favor of your business or detrimental to its activities.

- Noting counterintuitive data. Counterintuitive data is surprising or not what you would expect out of evaluating specific trends or making comparisons. Like anomalies, such information needs to be analyzed to determine whether or not they are favorable to the runnings of the business or detrimental to it.

It is essential that you take this time initially to do this analysis so that you realize the true goal of telling your data story rather than what you believe it to be. Analyzing data is quite an adventure as it can bring up unexpected twists and turns.

Step 2 - Align Your Data Story Goal with Your Audience

This step aligns with creating the setting, like in a fictional novel or a movie. It sets up the who and when of your data story. The "Who" is your audience. To tell a data story relevant to your audience, you need to take the time to learn about them. You need to understand factors such as their:

- Demographic
- Age
- Knowledge of the subject matter that will be prominent in your presentation
- Careers and educational background

Knowing these details and more allows you to develop your data story in a way that is most relatable to your listener. This will allow you to see if you can add more specific jargon to your data story or if you need to simplify the language for clearer takeaways while you are presenting. More importantly, knowing your audience allows you to understand why they care about the problem and the most specific solutions.

Knowing your audience allows you to develop the *when* of your data story. The "when" describes how far back the information needs to be provided and what current analysis and future predictions are specific and relevant to that group. These are the specific types of information that will be included in your data story to have the most impact on this group.

Step 3 - Develop the Structure of Your Data Story

With your audience and goal in mind, you can start developing the structure of your narrative. This structure will include the following elements:

1. The context of your data story. This speaks to why the story is relevant and worth telling to your audience. Knowing the context of your story allows you to develop a hook that engages your audience and makes them invested in it from the get-go.
2. The key players that are related to the context of that data story. Like in a book or movie, some characters are significant to the advancement of that story. These players could be executives, customers, clients, and more.
3. The problem that needs solving. The problem stated in your story is the whole reason this presentation was necessary in the first place. There is a conflict that your audience is invested in, and you need to state this clearly so that this group knows why they are being presented with this data.
4. The solution to the problem. Of course, if there is a problem, you cannot leave it unsolved. So, the

follow-up to letting your audience know what the problem is to provide them with possible solutions. These solutions need to be broken down into clear action steps that can be taken to solve this problem. You also need to provide your audience with this solution in a relatable way that allows them to know what value they are gaining by following the action solutions you have provided instead of other solutions.

It is best to tell your data story linearly. Following the structure from context to key players, and then problems and solutions. Just like you would not tell a story in a book or movie by starting with the middle or the end, you also need to deliver your data story in a way that makes sense to your audience.

Step 4 - Consider Your Visualizations

This is the climax of your data story. When you get to this point in your data story, you should be able to tick off your ultimate goal in having created that story in the first place. Your data visualizations bring all the previous elements together in a small flow that engages your audience and allows you to retain their attention so that you can deliver the climax of your data story, which is the solution to the problem.

Data storytelling is not just about *telling* your audience. You need to *show* your audience, and that is the role of creating visualizations. Visualizations enhance the story you are telling and help simplify the information so that the most important parts are highlighted clearly and immediately.

Remember that the visuals that you choose need to be relevant and engaging to your particular audience and be relevant to the insights being presented. These visuals need to capture their attention immediately *and* hold onto it for the duration of your presentation.

Infographics vs. Data Visualization

On the topic of data visualizations, it is pertinent that we take the time to address a point where many people feel confused. The fact is whether or not data visualizations and infographics are the same. The answer to that is they are not one and the same even though they are similar types of visual content.

Data visualizations are translations of datasets through individual charts that make that data easy to understand in a visual format. Whereas looking at massive spreadsheets with figures upon figures can be confusing, using data visualizations like a bar chart or a scatter plot allows you to digest that information in a much easier, faster way.

The purpose of infographics is to allow persons to note a large amount of information through the combination of text, icons, data visualizations, and illustrations to make an informed decision. As you can note from this definition, infographics include the use of data visualizations. Whereas data visualizations are typically brief visual content that communicates a certain point, infographics allow more information to be condensed in an organized flow. It is typical to note the use of infographics in areas such as the homepages of websites, landing pages for marketing campaigns, brochures, and social media.

Both of these types of visual content can have quite an impact when presenting data. However, which one you use depends on the purpose of the presentation. Infographics are typically used in marketing campaigns. Data visualizations are more prominently used for data storytelling.

. . .

You CAN SEE how crucial it is to present the right information in the right way. That is why developing your narrative is the first and, frankly, one of the most important elements of presenting data.

Now that we have developed our narrative let's move on to identifying, and captivating our audience.

2
CAPTIVATING YOUR AUDIENCE

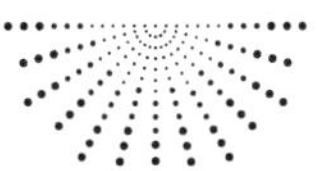

"Presentations aren't about the presenter; they're about the audience and what the audience needs."

— *SIMON RAYBOULD*

By now, you would have realized that your data story presentation's success depends on the depth of knowledge that you have about your audience. You need to have a profile of these people before you take even the first step in putting your information together and certainly before you start designing that presentation. Doing otherwise is like hunting in the dark and hoping to hit the target - a nearly impossible task.

Ensure that you hit the mark as close to the bullseye by putting in that preliminary groundwork about the people you will be presenting to. Ensure that you captivate these people to have the highest chance of eliciting the change you want from making that presentation.

The question that has many business professionals abandoning this vital task is the *how* of it. How exactly do you go about finding what you need to know about your audience so that you cater your data story to touch their emotions and better get your point across?

Luckily, this is not a matter of guesswork. You can implement proven methods to gather the information you need to know about this group. This chapter focuses on the "how" of getting this information and using it to maximum effect.

IDENTIFYING YOUR AUDIENCE

There are many questions that you can ask and, therefore, develop answers about your audience. However, just as you can get bogged down by the many bytes of data you want to convey to your audience, you can also get overwhelmed by the sheer number of questions you can ask about them. That does not have to be your reality. The solution here is to keep things as straightforward as possible.

Some important factors to consider are:

Job title. Knowing this will help determine what information they have access to frequently and the most important tasks they're involved in on a day-to-day basis. Knowing your audience's baseline knowledge can make or break your presentation.

Literacy level: Knowing your audience's literacy levels will greatly determine how you convey the information. Some common literacy levels are:

Analytical: Loves the fine details and data-driven solutions. Great at making sense of the data on their own. Show them as much valuable information as possible.

Competitive: Very fast-paced, motivated individual. Usually wants valuable insights they can act on, and they want them quick—no room for fluff.

Amicable: Very patient individuals. They love to discuss different avenues of action and the best possible solution to optimize the business's trajectory. It's worth having multiple possible solutions and lots of extra insights, showcasing different courses of action.

Don't ignore the importance of a simple personality type when presenting data.

Although all this background work can be rather tedious ill leave you with a quote to shift your perspective:

> "Give me six hours to chop down a tree and i will spend the first four sharpening the axe"
>
> — ABRAHAM LINCOLN

Who Is Your Audience?

The answer to this gives your audience a face. It makes you feel like you are talking to real people while compiling your data and preparing the visuals to support your message. This will undoubtedly help you build a better presentation compared to having an obscure image in your mind of what this group of people looks like.

With the power of knowing what your audience "looks" like, you are better able to shape a message that will be received by that audience.

There are five main categories of audiences that you will encounter as a data storyteller. They are:

The Novice

This is the type of audience's first exposure to the subject matter. In such a case, you want to simplify the information so that it is easy to understand. Therefore, jargon and technical terms should be avoided. Be very clear, concise, and informative. Focus on guiding them from knowing very minimal to understanding the entire sequence of events regarding the data.

The Generalist

This type of audience is more aware of the topic of discussion but still lacks understanding in certain areas. As the data storyteller, it is your job to fill in these gaps and provide this audience with knowledge on the major themes connected to the data being conveyed.

The Manager

Such an audience has an in-depth, actionable understanding of intricacies and interrelationships about the data due to their experience and access to details. As a data storyteller, you do not have as much to do concerning explanations, but that still does not take away the importance of conveying your message to this group in an efficient and effective manner. The manager will want straight to the point, yet valuable insights.

The Executive

This audience understands the importance and probable outcomes of certain situations but still needs the details. It is your job as the data storytelling to build the bridge between the data and those possible outcomes.

The Expert

This audience has the most in-depth knowledge about the data and does not rely as heavily on your presentation to be informed. This group is more interested in gaining more information compiled in a cohesive way to generate faster conclusions about the data.

Identifying your audience's job title and the depth of their knowledge of the data allows you to develop a strategy for how specific you need to be when explaining terms and designing your visuals. For example, a novice audience to the marketing strategy might need a rundown on the marketing budget allocation before they can understand why advertising performance is dropping. At the same time, a group of marketing managers or media buyers do not require such an explanation as they most likely will be familiar with the marketing budget. Knowing what your audience already knows determines how your data story will play out for the most effective communication. Keep in mind, being a novice doesn't mean it's their first day on the job. A higher-level executive might be unfamiliar with the new advertising strategy and needs a simple explanation to understand your point entirely.

Knowledge of your audience and understanding of the data also allows you to know what the listener is trying to gain from your data story.

Let's have a look at an example together and see how we would present to a specific audience.

In this case, we are presenting a product pricing recommendation for our new product launch. We had to consult the product manager for a potential price point change. They have very versatile knowledge of the product and were very motivated to launch, making them a competitive and analytical audience. The product manager and product team briefly determined the price point based on the average pricing of similar product launches in the industry. with further research, the product's initial pricing has changed over time and come to a new average price point. Our launch price needs to be corrected to be competitive. In this case, our audience knows many small details, so we want to be very straightforward with our data. Visualize the data in an easy-to-understand way that shows where we initially were pricing, where the competitors ended up, and our new recommended price point.

Before you compile your visual, we determined:

- Who: Product Manager ("The Manager, The Expert")
- What: Product launch price change

Now let's create this in visual form and present it.

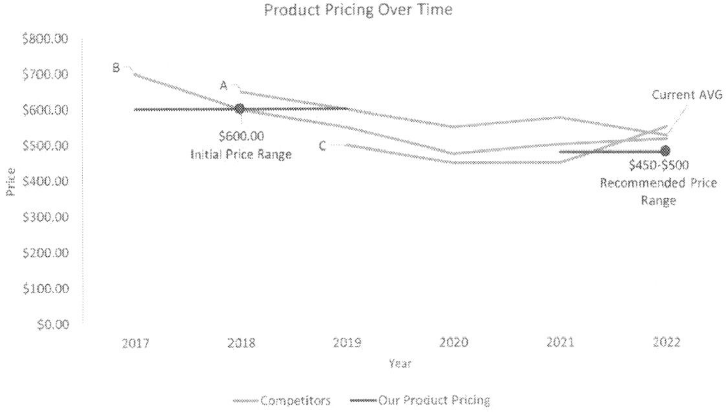

FIGURE 0.9- If you would like to follow along with a full color PDF, please join my email list at ElizabethSClarke.com and respond to the first email. I will happily send you the PDF version of the book.

"Our further research showed a trend in many companies initially pricing the product at an average of $600 (which was our initial price range) but reducing overtime to reach the industry sweet spot of $520, which is where we should be closer to. As you can see, At a price range of $450-$500, we fall just under the industry average to be competitive yet still in our desired gross profit margin of 50-60%."

This audience already knew the fine details, and all they needed was a quick and clear recommendation followed by some data to back it up. They can see the validity of this on their own.

(We will be dissecting this chart in chapter 4 and showcasing how we designed it for success)

Now, let's try this example again but for a different audience. We are the product manager, explaining why we selected this price point to the executives. They are busy with the big picture tasks within the overall company but aren't as in tune with individual product launches and details. This makes them an "executive" audience type. They needed to be filled in about how we got to this point.

Let's go over the questions to ask ourself:

- Who: CEO and executives ("The Executive")
- Literacy Level: Analytical
- What: Why we landed on the specific price point, and will it hit our desired targets.

The chart we used above will be valuable and effective. But with the audience having less knowledge of the details, they want to know why you landed on such a price point. We will need a few more slides to get them there.

When it comes to executives, their main focus is money. So let's show them why this price point will be effective and profitable. In this instance, A horizontal bar graph showing the profit % value can be effective. This way, the executives see what they want right away.

We can show how the costs and gross profit make up the overall price point. We can also compare it to our other products and their profit margins. Our company strives for a 60% gross profit margin for each product. Let's say our product is priced right in the middle of our price range at $475, with our cost at $204. We are left with $271, 57% gross profit. Which is right where we want it to be.

Let's visualize it!

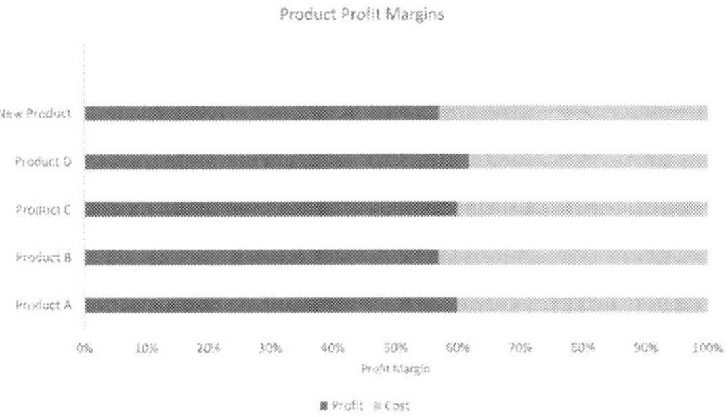

FIGURE 0.10

"Here is an overview of the gross profit margins for our top 4 products compared to our new product about to be launched."

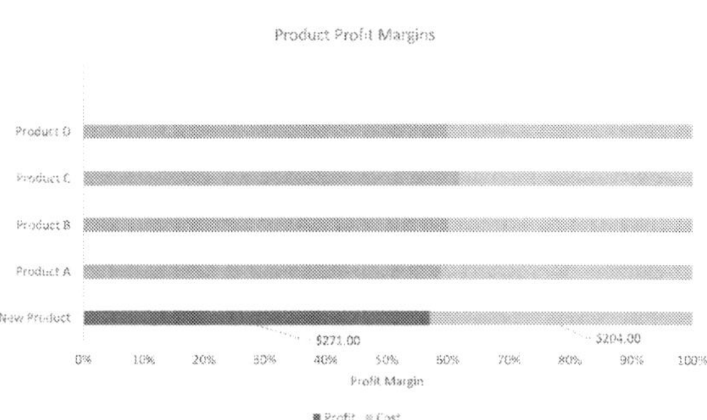

FIGURE 0.11

"As you can see, with our cost at $204, and a price point of $475, we are left with $271 (57%) profit which is right where we want to be."

"Let's have a look at how we ended up here."

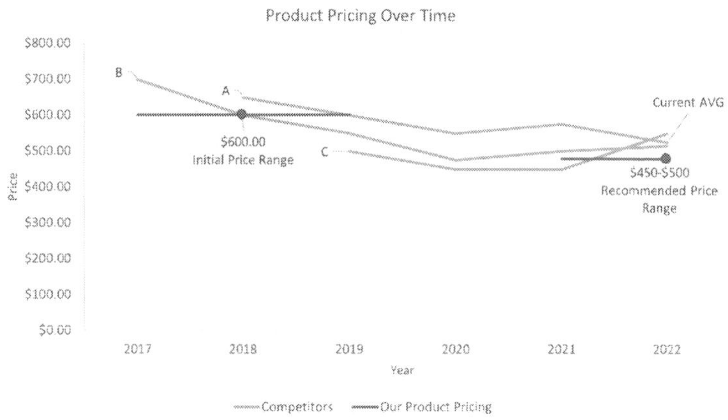

FIGURE 0.12

"*As you can see on the chart, Our initial price range was $600. The price was determined by the launch pricing average of our competitors. We discovered that the price points fluctuated over the last few years and landed at an average of $520. If we go with the $475 price point, we can sustain our desired profit margins while being the most competitive option.*"

By guiding the executives through the whole story and using attentive attributes to place their attention (We will talk more about attentive attributes later in the book), they can easily understand the reasoning behind your decisions and fully support your solution.

THE IMPORTANCE OF LANGUAGE

Judging how well your audience relates to the data that you will represent is very much related to the language you use. For example, if you are presenting to IT professionals about an IT-related subject, then this audience's literacy and numeracy literacy concerning IT-related subjects will be one where you do not have as much explaining to do. On the other hand, you may be presenting IT data to an audience made up primarily of HR representatives, and even if this group of people has excellent overall literacy and numeracy literacy aptitude, this group may find it challenging to understand the particular language, both literature, and numeral, relating to that subject matter. Similarly, if you are telling a data story about HR metrics, IT professionals may not have as high of a literacy and numeracy level to understand that particular language. In either case, you need to break the data down into manageable bite-sized pieces that are easy for the audience to digest.

Many business professionals are wary of approaching an audience with a lower literacy in that particular subject area, but this is instead an opportunity in disguise. See, the thing is, the actual mettle of a data storyteller is not made by how aesthetically pleasing their visualizations are or how well they put all the data together. Instead, this mettle is proven by how well this person can get the audience to follow their train of thought. Suppose you can get an audience with no prior knowledge of a subject area to understand that subject area. In that case, you deserve the title of a true professional data storyteller. Do not worry if you do not quite live up to that title yet, as this is a learned skill rather than one that some people are born with.

Some of the techniques that you can use to better improve the understanding of an audience that might have a lower literacy or number literacy levels include:

Avoid Using Technical Jargon as Much as Possible

All industries and niches have a unique language with acronyms and technical terminologies that will confuse outsiders who are not as familiar with the happenings of that setting. This particular language is called jargon. The last thing you want to do is leave your audience confused when they exit your presentation. Therefore, the best practice is to avoid using unique languages unless your audience is made up of people familiar with that industry or niche.

When it is necessary to use technical jargon with a novice audience, ensure that you take the time to explain what the terms mean and how they relate to the context of the presentation.

Be Humble and Use Humor

One of the best ways to break down jargon is to use humor. A good joke to break the ice is a great way to make everyone feel comfortable, yourself included. Humor is also an excellent tool for ensuring that your audience sees you as a person just like them and not someone talking down to them because of your superior knowledge of the data.

Be sure to convey through language and body language that you are willing to explain things that are unclear to your audience. When presenting a data story, the aim is not to impress your audience with how smart or informed you are. Instead, it is to inform your audience to make a sound decision about how to act thereafter. That means using language that the audience understands.

Pay Attention to Your Audience's Cues

There may be times when your presentation does not immediately resonate with your audience. This does not automatically mean a failed data story. Instead, you can learn to read the nonverbal cues that your audience expresses to adjust your language for effective communication to take place. Simply use a conversational tone to explain whatever information that you just imparted.

Reading the room is a skill that you *must* develop, as data storytelling is fluid and requires you to change and adjust on the spot to reach your audience no matter the circumstances.

Use the Power of Storytelling to Invoke an Emotional Response

Human beings love stories. It is why we read fiction novels and watch movies. It is why we cannot help but be engrossed by the dilemmas going on in other people's lives. It will also help many audiences, especially those composed of amicable and expressive audience members, feel more connected with you and, by extension, your data story. Relating your data to stories can give the audience a better mental visualization of the information you are trying to get across.

Allow Your Data Visualizations to Help Explain Technical Information

Of course, your verbal communication needs to be top-notch to reach your audience effectively. Any written paraphernalia you hand to your audience must also be relayed as professional, easy-to-understand content. However, you need to keep in mind that the human brain more easily deciphers visual content. Therefore, you need to take full advantage of the potential that your data visualizations afford you. This extends across the board and allows you to break down technical language into concise communication.

Focus on the Information That Is Relevant to Your Audience

All the parts of the data involved in your presentation might be fascinating to you. However, you have to remember that your audience is here for a particular reason, and things that you find fascinating might fail to capture the attention of your audience when that information ranges out of that scope.

Therefore, it is best that you highlight the things that your audience finds informative and relates to. For example, you might be presenting to an audience of marketing specialists who want to understand more about media buying. Such a presentation should focus on the process rather than its history or old tactics media buyers previously used.

HOW TO CAPTIVATE YOUR AUDIENCE

No matter how well of a package you have put together to develop your data story, if your audience does not get on board with your vision by finding that data helpful or fascinating, your call-to-action will be left unanswered. Luckily, there are a few techniques that you can use to up your chances of making that vital connection to keep your audience informed and decisive about the following steps to take.

The rest of this part includes nine key strategies for engaging your audience so that your data story is a fruitful one.

Focus on Connection Rather Than Making an Impression

Of course, you want to be seen as knowledgeable and authoritative as you deliver your data story to your audience. You want to make a great first and lasting impression. You want to wow these people. You want to be memorable. There is nothing wrong with such wants. However, they should not be your first priority.

Focusing on making a good impression with your audience makes your data story about you, when first and foremost, it should be about your audience and what they need to gain out of the presentation. Your audience needs to be changed in some way that is valuable to them by the time you say the last word of your data story. That change may be that they are now informed in a way that they were not before. It may be that they now understand the process of making a more informed decision in the future. It may be that they now understand data they did not previously. Any of these positive changes are aided by your hand, and so, your audience will develop a positive connection with you and your data story.

That should be your focus - building a positive connection rather than making a good impression. The best thing is that by prioritizing that connection, you up your chances of making that good impression.

Have a Strategic Plan

With all the bytes of data that you need to wade through to develop clear key points to deliver to your audience, sharing all that you know can seem more straightforward. That urge will be especially strong if your focus is to impress your audience with your knowledge. Your audience will not be impressed by data dumping. Instead, they are more inclined to feel overwhelmed and confused.

Avoid this by developing a strategy for turning all that data into key insights that develop the message you need to give to your audience. Think of the one thing that you want your audience to take away from your data story and develop a story and visuals to support that. Be as clear and as concise as possible as you do this. Everything that goes into your presentation needs to add to this core message. If it does not, remove it from your data story.

Bring Life to Your Data Story With Your Excitement

The first person who needs to feel enthused about your data story is you. If you are bored while thinking about it or while preparing the story, then the chances are that boredom will extend to your audience. You need to get fired up about your presentation to transfer that energy to your audience.

This excitement should not be faked, however. Your audience will feel that energy right away, and the effect will be the same. They will not be excited about your presentation any more than you are. Instead, add life to your story by infusing some of your personality through the use of your natural body language, facial expressions, changes in intonation and pace in your voice, and eye contact. Just remember to not go overboard with this. The personality type of your audience will dictate just how much of your personality you add to your data story. For example, a dry joke here and there will suffice with an analytical audience, while full-blown jokes may get to the heart of an expressive audience.

No matter the audience type, though, if you are rigidly delivering your presentation in a monotone voice and standing in the exact same position the entire time, you will lack the upbeat energy necessary for transferring excitement to your audience.

Use Stories to Make Your Data Story Unique

One sure way to add excitement to your data stories is to use your storytelling skills. The use of stories makes numbers and figures relatable. There is a time and place for hitting people with hard facts and figures. It is even appropriate at times during your data story. However, continually hitting your audience between the eyes with figures and hard facts will leave them lost. Soften the blow with stories. Not only do stories soften the blow, but they also make the data relatable, memorable, and more digestible to the audience.

Stories can come from anywhere that is appropriate to your data. They can be your personal experiences. They can be real-life examples that marry well with the data. Even jokes can be used to tell stories. Just remember to make these stories relevant to the data. An effective approach is to craft a story related to the data and convey it throughout the presentation to give context. People remember stories a lot better than they do numbers.

Use the Sandwich Approach to Highlight Key Insights

There will be a few key insights that support the main point of your data story. These insights are then supported by data points. Using such a structure allows you to know what is relevant to present to your audience.

A strategy called the Sandwich Approach promotes the stating of insight followed by delivering relevant data to support the insight. The insight is then repeated to reinforce that information. Think of the insight as the pieces of bread on the top and bottom of the sandwich and the data as the filling to complete the sandwich. The intended effect is to show the audience how the data is relevant to the keep points that they will be taking away from the data story.

I'll use an example to explain further how to utilize this tactic. Let's say you have some metrics you need to present that look like this:

- According to our metrics, our company's data growth will be 300% higher in 2022 than in 2018.
- Our data collection spending is expected to reach $50,000 in 2021.
- Only 2% of our companies data is being analyzed.
- Only 27% of our data projects have been labeled as "successful."
- 61% percent of our executives admit that we have a long way to go to use company data properly.

A clear insight would be:

Insight: We know that our data is growing rapidly, but the fact of the matter is we are not using it effectively.

Data: Data growth will be 300% higher in 2022 compared to 2018, reaching an estimated spend of $50,000 this year.

This being said, only 2% of our data is being analyzed, and that which is being analyzed is not necessarily helping our organization: Only 27% of our data projects have been labeled as "successful." while 61% percent of executives admit that we have a long way to go in using company data properly.

Insight: So, even though our data is growing, figuring out how to use it effectively will help us have the cutting edge in our industry.

Structuring your insights this way helps the audience to better understand what they need to know. The initial problem, some data to back up that point, and reiterating the initial takeaway/solution. Hence, "sandwiching" the data between two insights, so the data has an introduction and conclusion instead of an open end. The clarity of this method is far superior than a list of information.

Avoid Vague Generalizations

You need to be specific and concise when delivering figures and hard facts about your data. As mentioned earlier, there is a time and place to soften the impact of numbers and facts, but when you do indeed deliver them, do not be wishy-washy about the act. Deliver them so that impact is immediate and deliberate.

You might be worried about overwhelming your audience when you make these deliveries, but the way to avoid this is to ensure that you are not delivering fluff. Any information that you make part of your data story needs to earn its place there. It needs to contribute to the insights and ultimately to the core message of the presentation. Trim the data down to the minimum and deliver it comprehensively.

Spreadsheets... Don't Use Them in Your Data Story

Spreadsheets are beautiful things that help us compile, calculate, and track data. They are a necessary tool for making sense of the many many bytes of data created every day. As useful as spreadsheets are to you as a data analyst, they are not something you should deliver to your audience. Think of it as being the director of a movie. You do not show your audience the script or any of the other raw products used to make that movie. Rather, you present the final product, which will educate or entertain. The same analogy needs to apply to data storytelling.

Your job as the data storyteller is to use that information to design a final product that allows the audience to easily comprehend the relevant data which has already been compiled, calculated, and tracked.

Use Trends and Patterns

Imagine having thousands of small balls of all different colors sent at you simultaneously and being told to catch only blue ones in less than 1 minute. An overwhelming and impossible task, correct? This is essentially the situation that some data storytellers present their audience with.

Being presented with many small pieces to a whole and then being asked to put the pieces together is a formidable task, especially when they are millions of pieces. Your audience is coming to you to avoid this overwhelm, and the best way to facilitate that path of easy understanding is by compiling relevant pieces of data into trends and patterns. In essence, you will be putting all the blue balls together, all the green balls together, and so on.

Trends and patterns allow the audience to grasp how the data is developing over time and what predictions can be made for the future from the present and past data. This facilitates more informed decision-making.

Leave Your Audience With Practical Advice and Takeaways

As I said earlier, the mark of a good data storyteller is leaving the audience with a positive change by the end of a presentation. Do not leave this up to chance, though. Make it easy for your audience to know what you want them to take away from the data story so that they can start acting immediately to make good on your call to action. Give them a detailed outline of how they can use the information they gather from you to pave a better way forward.

HOW TO KNOW IF YOU HAVE GOT IT RIGHT WITH YOUR AUDIENCE

Unfortunately, there is no way of knowing whether or not you have hit the nail on the head with your audience until you are in the thick of things while presenting. This is why it is so important that you do the preliminary work necessary for gathering information about this audience and how best to approach them with your data. We've analyzed the data, we know what it means. It's now our job to persuade and guide our listeners to the proper business decisions.

Do not despair if you do not quite get it right with your audience. There is no such thing as a failed presentation. What there is are business professionals who fail to learn lessons when things do not go quite their way. Analyze how every presentation goes. Gather data about it. As much as I would love to tell you all there is to know about getting it right with your audience, a lot of it boils down to experience. You have to act and note the results from each experience. The more knowledge you gather under your belt, the more you will be able to fine-tune your skills to connect with your audience the next time and the time after that.

Now that we have identified our audience, we will know what information needs to be presented, and with that information, we can select the proper charts. Let's move on to that now.

3
REFINING YOUR VISUALS - CHOOSING THE RIGHT CHART

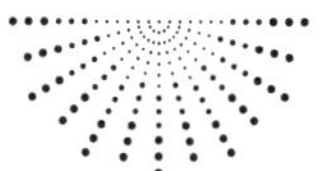

"Data visualization is the language of decision making. Good charts effectively convey information. Great charts enable, inform, and improve decision making."

— *DANTE VITAGLIANO*

So, you have done it. You have taken the time to develop your narrative and find out who exactly you're presenting to. With those two crucial steps out of the way, you now know what information must be presented.

However, no matter how grand your narrative is, there needs to be something that attracts your audience to the data that you have to present. Think of it like this, many people say that we should not judge a book by its cover. But guess what? Most of us do, as we rightly should because first impressions are often correct.

The charts that you choose represent what your audience's first impression will be. Those visuals will draw your audience in for a further examination of what this represents or what will turn them away. Your visualizations need to correlate with the type of data that you are presenting to that audience. It is what will make that data understandable and, therefore, engaging to your audience.

Because data visualizations are such a massive part of making the most impact on your audience, it only fits that those visuals have the spotlight in this chapter. Therefore, the coming pages will focus on the importance of balanced visuals that genuinely represent the narrative of your data story and why it is vital to choose the correct chart, and how to do so.

THE IMPORTANCE OF VISUAL REPRESENTATION

The sense of sight. It is one that we often take for granted, even though it is what we most heavily rely on—approximately 90% of the information that our brains process daily is provided via sight. Most of how we interpret and interact with the world around us results from what we see.

The process that happens from the time we see something to the brain processing what this visual means is called visual perception. It describes the process of the brain analyzing and then interpreting the information it gains from our sight. This process happens so quickly - in an average of only 13 milliseconds - that it is easy for us to discredit the importance that it plays in our daily lives.

Of course, visual perception is a vital process that has allowed the continuation of the human species. Still, it is also essential that you understand how this process can enhance your data story. The human brain processes visual information far faster than textual images - 60,000 times faster, in fact.

I am not just providing these statistics to enhance your mental muscles. I am providing these small tidbits of data to show you that the visual aspect of your data story can be processed far faster than any bit of text that you think to provide to your audience. The human brain is better acclimated to seek out and process visuals, so the many bytes of data can be conveyed to your audience better in this way.

Often pictures speak louder than words. When giving your presentation, you need a powerful visual representation that supports the strong narrative you should have developed beforehand. If you take the time and use the resources available to you to create appropriate and visually impactful charts, your visualizations should allow for:

More Information in Less Space

Here is a comparison for you. It takes an average of almost 2 minutes to read one page of a book. Your brain can visually perceive the same information in that text format in mere milliseconds if presented as a chart.

Higher Engagement Rates

Creating good data visualizations is the one aspect of a data story that you can use to ensure that you not only capture your human audience's attention but also hold onto it for more than 8 seconds. However, you do not only want to capture and hold your audience's attention. You want to also make them feel invested in that data story. This will increase the chances of the audience engaging you for more context to the information being shared. Good visualizations have the power to gain you that objective.

A Higher Rate of the Audience Performing the Call-To-Action Delivered at the End of Your Presentation

With the increased engagement rate that good visuals provide, there is a higher probability that the audience will act in a way that aligns with the call-to-action that you will provide in the climax to your data story. The fact is that the more visually stimulated we are by something, the more emotionally attached we will become to that thing. From that comes the higher likelihood we are to act on these emotions. Therefore, translating your data into appropriate visuals allows your audience to respond quicker to the action steps that you provide in your data story.

Allows for a More Everlasting Effect

It will do you no good if your story is forgotten the minute your audience steps outside the room. You need to ensure that your presentation was impactful enough to stick in their memory. Your data story needs to have a lasting effect that encourages your audience to follow through with the call-to-action and perhaps convince others to participate in fulfilling their call-to-action.

Attractive and informative data visualizations give you the power to stick in your audience's memory and thus, increase engagement.

CHOOSING THE RIGHT CHART

So we have established the value of having attractive, engaging charts in your data story. However, the question remains - how do you choose the correct chart to align with your narrative and allow the natural progression from the problem to be solved? The anxiety that this problem can induce is only compounded when this data story requires multiple charts. How do you keep your message from being lost in the noise of using the wrong charts? How do you use data visualizations to enhance the content you are presenting rather than take away from its value?

Luckily, you can avoid the anxiety of these questions by following the advice provided in this section.

Choosing the correct chart starts with examining the narrative you have developed and then asking yourself what type of data is being represented. You will most likely be dealing with data falling in one of these four categories:

- Comparison
- Composition
- Relationship
- Distribution

Each of these types of data is best showcased by certain types of charts. Therefore, we will break down what each data type means and the charts typically best suited to make that representation.

Comparison

This data type shows how one set of data compares to at least one other group of data. With this type of data, there may be multiple variables from different sets of data or various categories within one data set. For example, if the data you are presenting focuses on salary comparisons, diverse datasets may show salaries within different science communities. On the other hand, a college may show salary variables in the various departments.

Data comparison is often used in data stories because it is simple in concept and application yet allows powerful results. Data comparison provides for:

- Tracking how data changes over time
- Showing the differences and similarities between different sets of data
- Showing the differences between past and current data
- Showing the results before and after solutions and applications have been applied

When making comparisons about particular items in relation to different sets of data, some of the best charts to use include:

- Column charts
- Bar charts
- Tables

When comparison data shows the movement over time, some of the best charts to use include:

- Line charts
- Column charts
- Circular area charts

Composition

This type of data allows noting how part of a data set can compare to the whole data set. Data stories that show composition can be static or show change over time. Also, composition data may be expressed in absolute numbers or in relative forms such as percentages to show the variations of parts of the whole. Just like comparison data, composition data is a widely used type of data.

Examples of visualizations that can be used to show static composition include:

- Pie charts
- Waterfall charts
- Column charts

In the case of composition data that changes over time, commonly used charts include

- Column charts
- Area charts

Relationship

This type of data shows the connection between at least two variables in a given set of data. An example of a relationship with only two variables may be children's height relative to their age. Another data set exploring relationships with multiple variables includes website conversions from specific demographics such as age, gender, etc.

If someone just dumped a bunch of numbers on you, there is no way of finding the correlation between these numbers until they are grouped to show relationships. Good visualizations help determine these relationships.

Scatter plots and bubble charts are typically used to show relationships in presentations. Scatter plots are more commonly used when there are only two variables, while bubble charts are more commonly used when there are more than two variables.

Distribution

Useful in developing trends, this type of data shows how variables in a set of data or multiple steps of data are distributed over time. With trends, probabilities can be developed to offer predictions of possible outcomes based on historical information. For example, data from a swim club may show that swimmers in different height categories swim at different paces. This data can be used to make future predictions as to who might be the top competitors based on different swim categories. Column charts, line histograms, scatter plots, and 3D area charts commonly show distribution data.

While these four types of data are considered the pillars of data visualization, there are more techniques that you can use to determine what is the right visuals appropriate for your particular data story. This, of course, involves asking yourself a few questions. One of the commonalities that you might have noticed mentioned in the types of data outlined above is the number of variables in datasets. Therefore, one of the first questions you need to ask yourself is how many datasets are represented and how many variables are outlined in each data set.

Once that has been determined, you also need to question how many data points will be displayed for each variable chosen to be outlined in that chart, as well as you need to determine whether or not these data points will be plotted over a period of time or another variable that shows progression or grouping.

Once you have adequately established the data type and answered the questions above, you can determine the best visualizations for that data story.

TYPES OF CHARTS AND WHEN AND WHY TO USE THEM

There are tons and tons of different types of charts that can enhance the narrative of data stories. There is no way that we can delve into all of them, but we can look at those that are more widely used. You must understand the basics of charts and how and when you can use them before you dive into the use of more complex visuals.

While there was nothing wrong with leaning on more complex charts when it is warranted (remember that balance between problem complexity and visual complexity), there is no disputing the fact that clean, simply-put-together charts can most often get your point across more efficiently and effectively when supported by a good narrative compared to more complex visuals. Again, this is subjective to the data story that you are presenting. Still, you need to know what the foundational charts are, and how, why, and when to use them before you go onto the use of complex graphs.

Some of the foundational charts that every good data storytelling need to know how to use include:

BAR GRAPHS

This type of chart has a lot of aliases. It also goes by the name of a column chart. It is so named because it allows data visualizations where numeric values are featured in the form of bars. The levels of these bars are plotted on one axis while the values are plotted on the other axis. Each category of data is highlighted on one axis, and the length of that bar corresponds to the value on the other axis. Bar charts can make use of either vertical or horizontal bars. The categories are placed on the horizontal axis when vertical bars are used, and the opposite is true when horizontal bars are used. Vertical bars are the norm, but horizontal bars are good practice when working with long category labels. Whether you use vertical bars or horizontal bars, the thing you need to ensure is that you accurately label each axis.

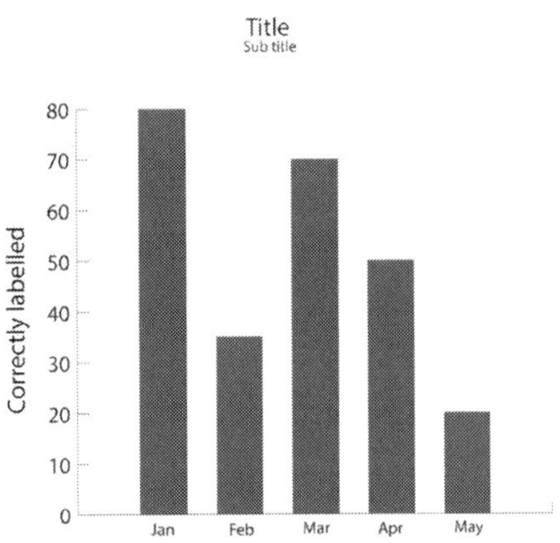

FIGURE 1 Bar graph

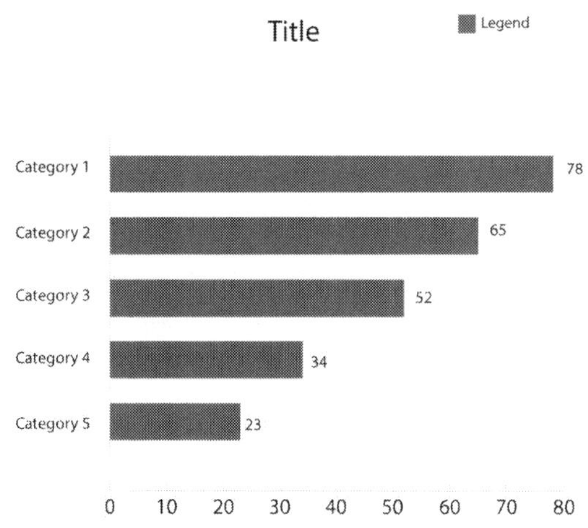

FIGURE 1.1 Horizontal bar graph

Another common type of bar chart is called the stacked bar chart. The name comes from the fact that individual bars are divided into sub-bars stacked on top of each other to show the correlation between different categories. For example, a marketing team may use a bar chart to compare their marketing budget from 2018-2020. The team will further break down each year in a stacked bar chart to show the budget allocation. The height of the bar will establish the total budget, and the bar will be divided into different sections showcasing the portion of the budget for that year.

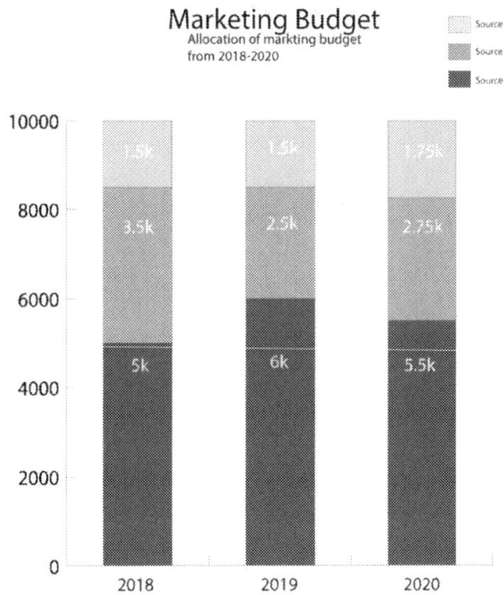

FIGURE 1.2 Stacked bar graph

Bar charts allow for the easy comparison of data variables, so bar charts are commonly used when comparing data types featured in a data story. However, bar charts are not just limited to show comparison data. They are also used to indicate the distribution of data points. So many data stories that showcase groups of highest or lowest, or most common to least common variables showcase bar charts.

To have the most impact when using bar charts in your presentation, there are a few rules that you should stick to. These rules include:

Consider Order of Values

Bar charts are commonly used to show comparisons and trends, and the standard conventionally is to place bar categories from longest to shortest. This allows the audience to interpret comparisons easily and to realize trends.

This rule is not hard set. If categories are inherently ordered in a specific way to serve a particular purpose, then that takes precedence over the longest to shortest ordering convention.

Use Rectangular Shapes

You might be tempted to get fancy when you are doing your bar charts but resist this temptation. Ensure that the shapes of your bar fit a rectangular form with straight edges. You might see rounded bar shapes used in some bar charts, but these types of bar charts can easily be misinterpreted as the audience will find it difficult to tell where the bar indicates the value on the axis.

Also, avoid using 3D bars, even if you might see these being more commonly used. Again, they make it difficult for the audience to interpret the bar's actual value and add unnecessary visual noise.

We will focus more on design in chapter 4.

PIE CHARTS

Pie charts are so commonly used in data visualization that some people might say that they are overused. We will delve into when it is appropriate to use pie charts and times when it is inappropriate. Also, we will look at how to determine what is proper and improper related to pie chart usage. However, before we get to that, let's look at pie charts and their value to data visualization.

Circular in nature, pie charts are data visualization tools that use slice sizes to depict parts of a whole or highlight the relationship between multiple datasets. Investors share percentage, for example.

The primary use of the pie charts is to compare the groups contained within one set of data. Suppose we reuse our investor share example from above. In that case, we can either develop one pie chart showcasing what percentage each investor owns. Or, we can create three separate pie charts to show each investors shares in relation to the whole. In this case, creating three different pie charts doesn't make all that much sense, and those two types of data cannot be compiled into the same pie chart as these data points would confuse your audience. Compilation is best done using bar charts.

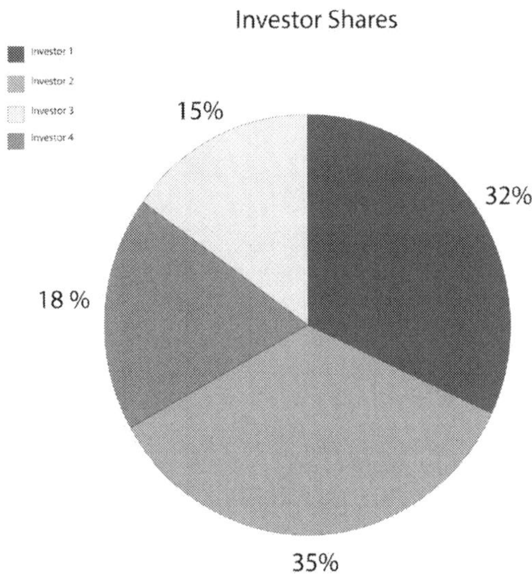

FIGURE 1.3 Non effective chart - Not the best option for this set of values as it is doesn't visually represent the data effectively or draw an easy conclusion.

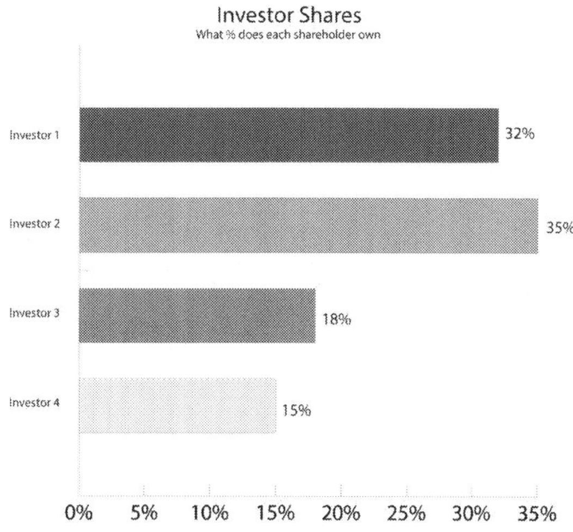

FIGURE 1.4 The more effective choice- A better option for this set of values as you can immediately distinguish who owns what % of shares in relation to each other.

Just as there are rules for creating the best bar charts possible when doing presentations, that also applies to the development of pie charts. Some of these rules include:

Use Annotations

It is often difficult to determine the exact proportion of each pie slice by sight alone. Do not burden your audience with the task of trying to make these determinations but using annotations. These annotations can take up the form of fractions, percentages, or whole numbers.

Use a Limited Number of Pie Slices

Can you imagine if you used a pie chart to present the budget allocation for an entire company? You would need a magnifying glass and lots of time on your hands to go over all that data. That is certainly not a task you want to give to your audience. Therefore, limiting the number of pie slices that make up your pie chart is essential. The use of five categories or less is the standard practice with pie charts. Creating a pie chart with more slices makes the visual look cluttered and hard to decipher. Coming back to our earlier example, if the values have a noticeable difference then it might work in your favor to use a pie chart. As you can easily distinguish who owns how much of the whole at a glance.

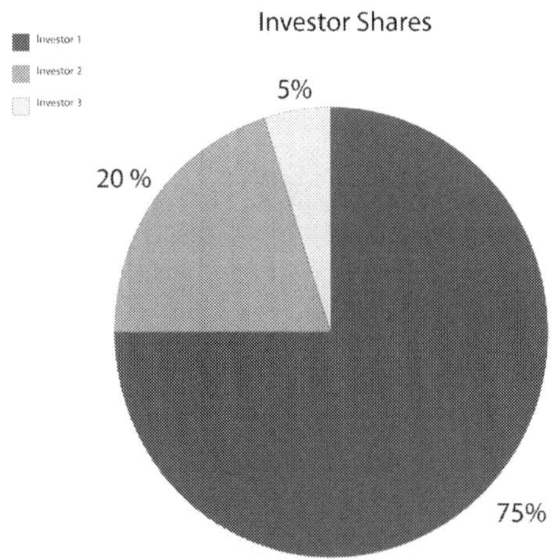

FIGURE 1.5 When to use a pie chart - If you have minimal values and can easily distinguish the parts of the whole, a pie chart may be an effective option.

Personally, if I need more than three or four categories, I'll switch to a bar chart. Pie charts are best used for a simple part of the whole analysis, nothing more. Even very few slices can aid confusion if the figures are similar to each other.

Order Your Pie Slice for Easy Reference

Like with bar charts, the order you choose to deliver your data can enhance the experience for your audience or detract from it. The standard practice is to order the slices from biggest to smallest. Also, just like with bar charts, that regular convention takes a backseat to inherent orders that allow for a better viewing experience.

Use Flat Shapes to Represent Pie Charts

The use of 3D shapes is becoming more and more popular in data visualization with the popularity of 3d modeling, but they leave too much room for misinterpretation. Avoid using anything apart from flat shapes that best show the proportion of data represented by a pie slice.

LINE GRAPHS

Also called a line chart or a line plot, a line graph is just what it sounds like. It is a type of data visualization that shows continuous progression using lines from left to right to show changes in value. This constant progress is shown on the chart's horizontal axis, while the vertical axis shows the value metrics that highlight that change. For example, a marketing agency might use a line chart to show how the website traffic from their top advertising campaigns for one of their clients has been distributed over the first 3 quarters going into Q4. The line will show the progression from January to September on the horizontal axis, while the vertical axis will show the metric value, which is the number of website visitors and how it differs throughout the first 3 quarter's. With this information they can see how their campaign performance is and note some possible projections going into Q4.

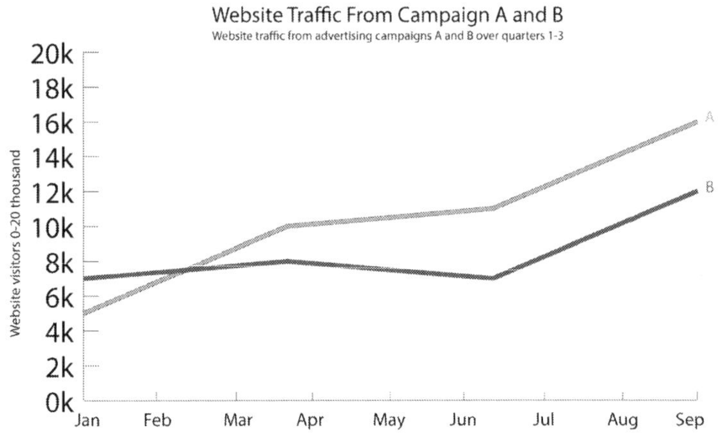

FIGURE 1.6 Comparison - An effective use of a line graph comparing the performance between campaign A and campaign B over the first three quarters.

Because of this structure, line charts are great for showing trends and distribution. To make the most out of the use of line charts, here are a few rules that you can stick to when creating them:

Choose Appropriate Measurement Intervals for Both the Horizontal and Vertical Axis

Also called a bin size, the proper interval between measurements plotted on both axes of a line chart is important for a quick and accurate interpretation of data. There is no strict science on how to choose an appropriate interval. Instead, this relies on your knowledge of the data and how best to translate it to the audience.

For example, if we go back to showing the website traffic for May, a daily interval on the horizontal axis is likely appropriate. On the other hand, this would be inappropriate for visitors over a year. Instead, a monthly interval would be more appropriate because it will be less tedious for your audience to read - 12 intervals rather than 365.

Limit the Use of Lines

More than one line can be used to show the progression on a line chart. For example, a marketing agency might have individual lines to show website visits, add to carts, or purchases over a year to track the conversions rates.

However, while multiple lines are great at highlighting certain pieces of data, too many lines can confuse your audience and lead to misinterpretation. As a rule of thumb, limit the number of lines used to 5 or less.

Limit the Use of Dual Axises

There are times when you will come across line charts with dual horizontal axes. For example, they may be used to show negative and positive values with the line progression. A company can use this to show an audience the periods when it makes a profit compared to when a loss was made over each month of one year.

While a dual-axis can enhance the understanding of your audience, this is typical in a point of confusion. Therefore, where it is possible to communicate the data without a dual-axis, do so even if it means using another chart type.

AREA CHARTS

A slightly more complicated chart is the area chat. What makes the area chart special is that it combines a bar chart and a line chart to show the progression of a variable compared to another set of data. This progression is usually demonstrated over intervals of time. The difference between a line chart and an area chart is the shading notable between the lines and the horizontal axis.

Area charts are typically used to show comparisons between multiple variables or how one set of data is divided into different proportions. Because of this, there are two main types of area charts.

The first one is called an overlapping area chart. This type of area chart shows the comparison between variables and different sets of data. This type of chart offers the standard line, but each point plotted on the vertical axis indicates the value for every variable in the different datasets. Each plot point has shading between the line and the horizontal axis. Of course, this shading can add a little panache to an area chart, but it shows the greatest value in each variable and differentiates each variable from the others. As a result, such a chart will typically be distinct as it has figures that look like mountain peaks. An example of an overlapping area chart could be monitoring website traffic during a product launch throughout the day from different sources.

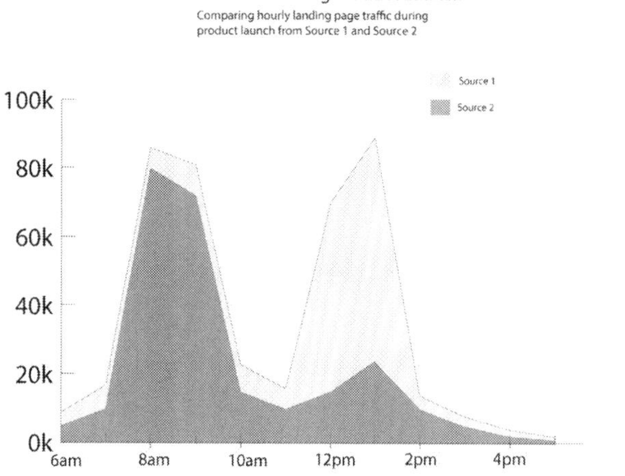

FIGURE 1.7 Comparing landing page traffic - Comparing website traffic from separate sources during a product launch. Can easily distinguish the better performing funnel to focus advertising on that specific source in the future.

While overlapping area charts are great for showing how different datasets correlate and are differentiated from each other, you should limit the number of data groups placed in one such chart. As a rule of thumb, limit the variables to three or less.

The second type of area chart is a stacked area chart, and it is used to show how individual categories of one set of data progress. Such a chart helps track a total value and break that one set of data down into separate categories. Such charts make use of multiple lines, and just like a stacked bar chart makes use of different colors to show subcategories, so does a stacked area chart.

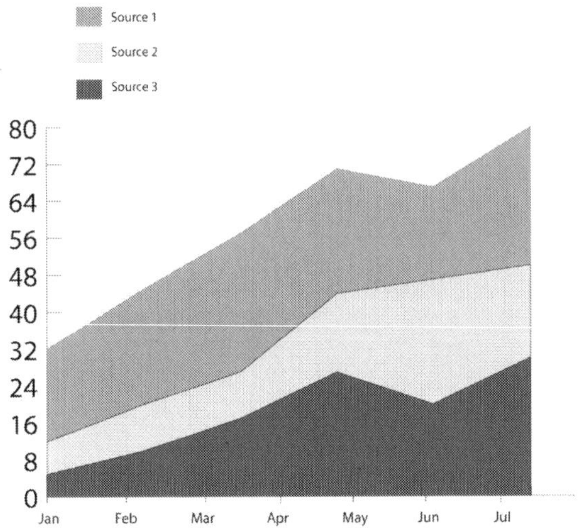

FIGURE 1.8 Stacked area chart - comparing trends over time while easily understanding each value amount.

An example of a stacked area chart would be an airport noting the number of persons entering the country and where each visitor is arriving from for the year.

SCATTER PLOTS

Mainly used to show the relationship between at least two variables, scatter plots use dots to represent values based on these variables and how they correlate in relation to one another. These points allow for reporting the relationship between two variables and show patterns in the distribution of that data.

The relationship between the plotted points can show various positive, linear, and strong patterns. Such a pattern shows the distribution of these dots in a line that has an upward trend. On the other hand, the distribution of dots may indicate no clear relationship between the two variables as these dots are plotted all over the chart. Of course, other relationships can be shown between these two extremes, such as one that is non-linear but still strong. To make the general trends that are developed by the plot points in this type of chart easy to spot, it is helpful to draw lines based on the distribution of those points. This line is known as a trend line.

Scatter plots are not just limited to the use of only two variables. A third variable can be added, but more variables are not recommended as this will lead to creating a cluttered chart that is hard to understand. The plotting of too many variables is called overplotting, and it is so-called because having too many variables and dots makes it challenging to understand the relationship between them.

As great as scatter plots are, there is one possible problem that you may run into when using them. While you can note the relationship between two variables, you cannot determine what causes this relationship based on the points plotted on a scatter plot. The counter to this limitation with this type of chart is that it invites further investigation.

Here are some examples of possible scatter plot outcomes:

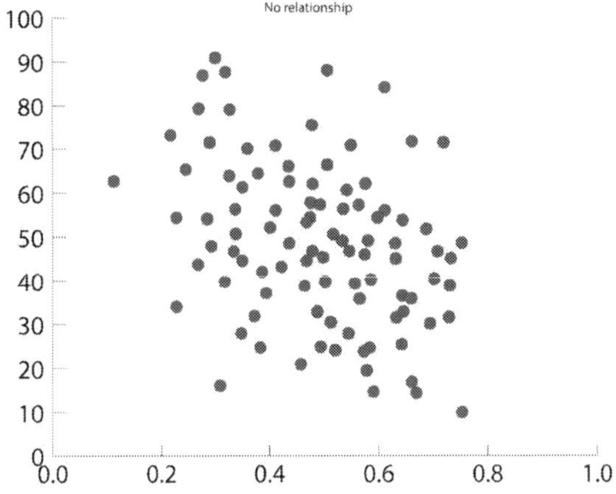

FIGURE 1.9 No relationship known.

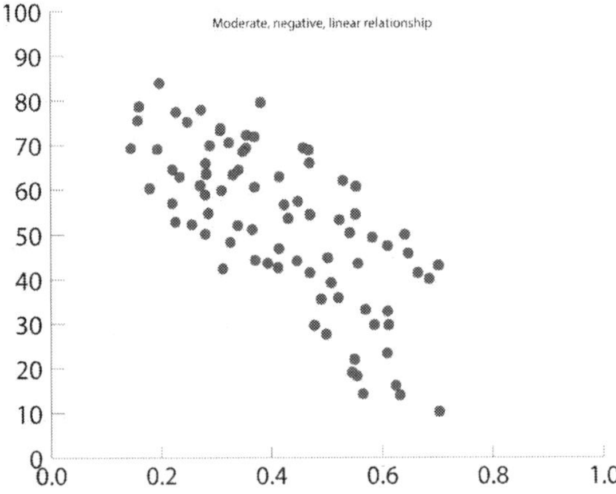

FIGURE 1.10 Moderate, negative, linear relationship.

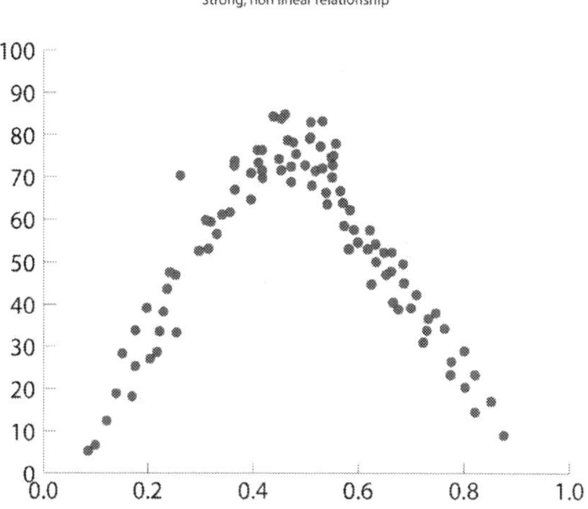

FIGURE 1.11 Strong, non linear relationship.

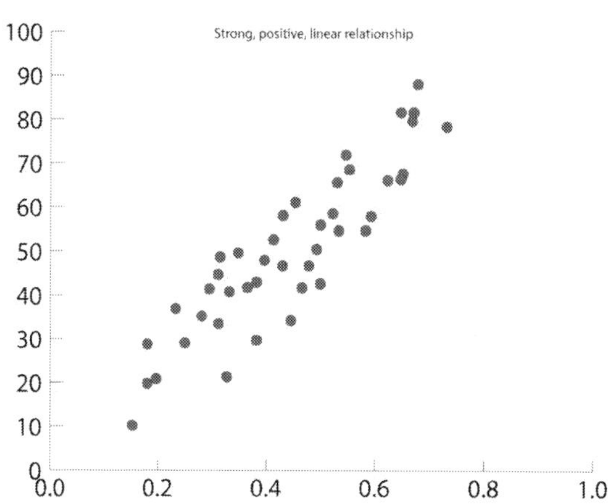

FIGURE 1.12 Strong, positive, linear relationship.

USING TABLES

At this point, I am sure that you might be wondering one thing - so, what about tables? Don't worry. I have not forgotten about them.

Tables are often the source of the data you will develop into visualizations throughout your career developing data stories. You might even find that they make good data visualizations when showcasing comparison, composition, and relationship data types. Especially when there are few variables or data points to be outlined to your audience.

Other times when it would be appropriate to use tables include:

- When the data cannot be easily represented in a visual format.
- When you need to showcase precise values to your audience or bring the audience's attention to unique datasets.
- When the data that needs to be communicated does not involve trends but is instead of a quantitative informative nature
- When the data involved has multiple units of measurement
- When making comparisons
- When you need to showcase individual values to your audience.
- When highlighting causes of the patterns shown in the data presented.
- When specific parameters need to be shown to highlight particular datasets.

Apart from that, charts are the best data visualizations to impress upon your audience the message contained within the data or when you want to highlight the relationship between datasets or groups within a dataset.

Of course, you are not limited to just the use of tables or just the use of charts. As long as the narrative of your story remains concise, use whatever visual properties you think will enhance your message.

WATERFALL CHART

A waterfall chart can be a great option for analytical purposes, especially for explaining and understanding the gradual transition in the value of something subjected to increment or decrement. A good example would be changing revenue or profit between two time periods. It essentially visualizes a running total as values are added or subtracted.

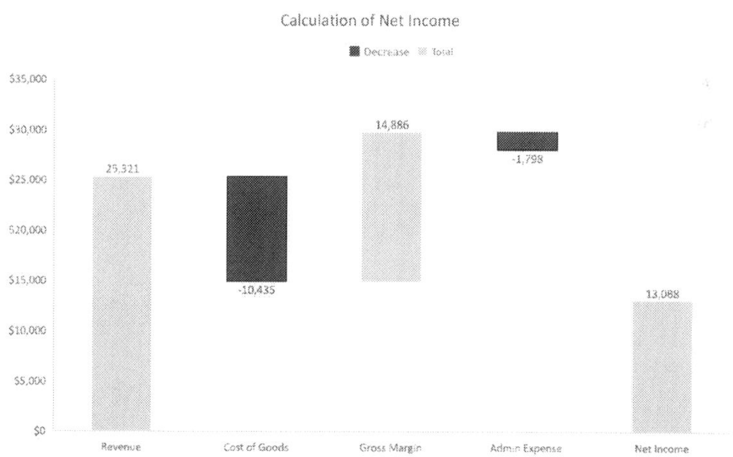

FIGURE 1.13- Waterfall chart calculating net income.

TREEMAP

Treemaps can be used when you want to visualize a part-to-whole relationship amongst a large number of categories. They are mainly used when direct comparisons between categories are not necessary. They allow for the quick perception of the items that are large contributors to each category.

Although treemaps are visually appealing, they can often be used when a different visualization might serve the data better. When encoding data with a large area and intensity of color, it can be hard for the audience to decipher minor differences. We should never make our audience do more work than necessary to understand a graph! Keep this in mind when using a treemap.

FIGURE 1.14- Treemap showcasing allocation of certain budgets.

FIGURE 1.15- Treemap showing parts of an operational budget.

HISTOGRAMS

Use histograms when you have continuous measurements and want to understand the distribution of values and look for outliers. These graphs take your continuous measurements and place them into ranges of values known as bins.

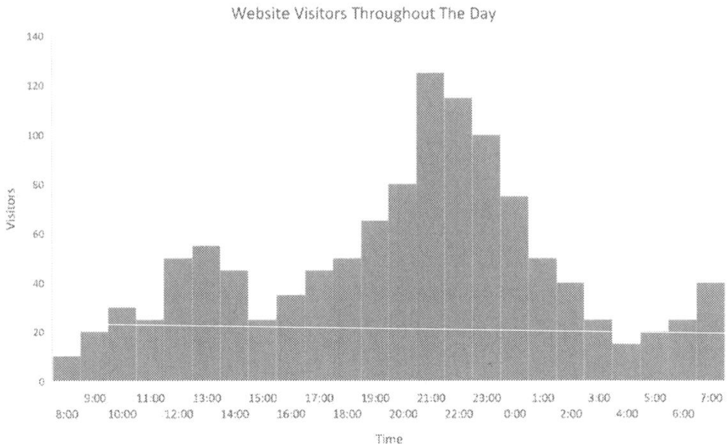

FIGURE 1.16- Histogram Showing website visitors over a 24 hour period.

FUNNEL CHART

Funnel charts are great for sequential data that moves through at least four stages.

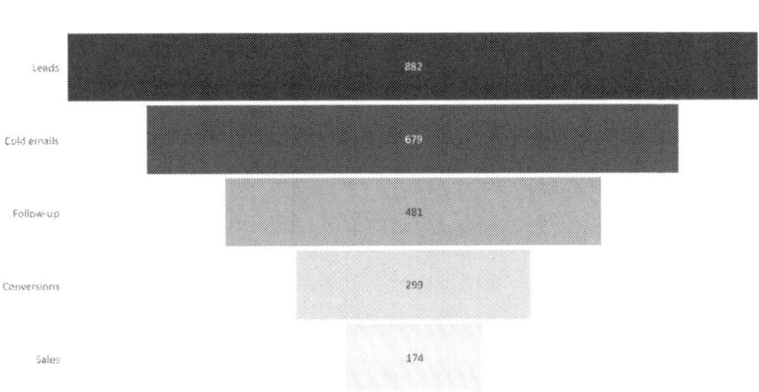

FIGURE 1.17- Funnel chart example.

How to Make Charts

Now that you have a better understanding of choosing the right charts to enhance your data story, you might run into *how* to create these charts. Although an in-depth guide will have to be saved for another book, I will point you in the right direction if you don't already have your tool of choice. Here are some top options:

- **Excel**

Excel is an industry-standard and my preferred method for creating visualizations. Data scientists working with code and more complex data sets might prefer programs like Tableau as it easily syncs with more extensive databases. But for many business situations, Excel is more than adequate. Excel might be straightforward for many business professionals, but i'll give you a quick rundown on creating and customizing charts with excel. Feel free to skip this if you're an Excel expert.

Simply highlight (Select) your data, then select the lightning bolt icon in the corner. You can hover over the desired charts to preview them.

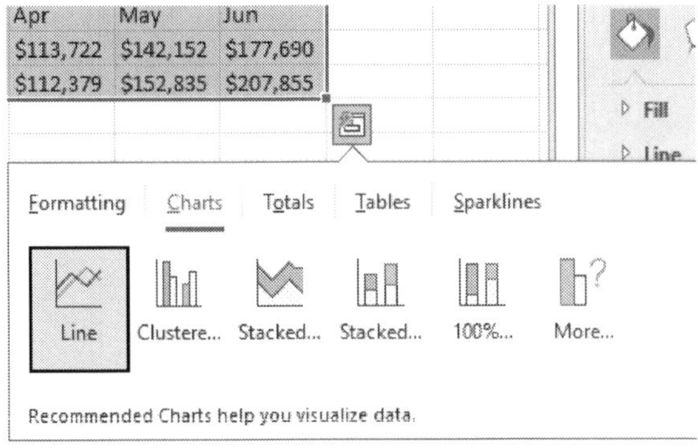

FIGURE 1.18

If you want to turn a set of data into a visualization easily, simply highlight your desired data, type ALT-F1, and it will auto-populate into a chart immediately.

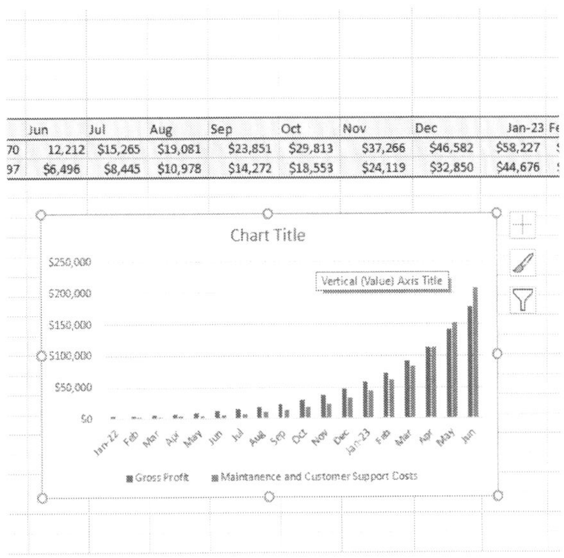

FIGURE 1.19

From there, under "Chart Design," you can select from many different chart types and design options to customize and make your own. You can also change the chart type by right-clicking on the middle of the chart.

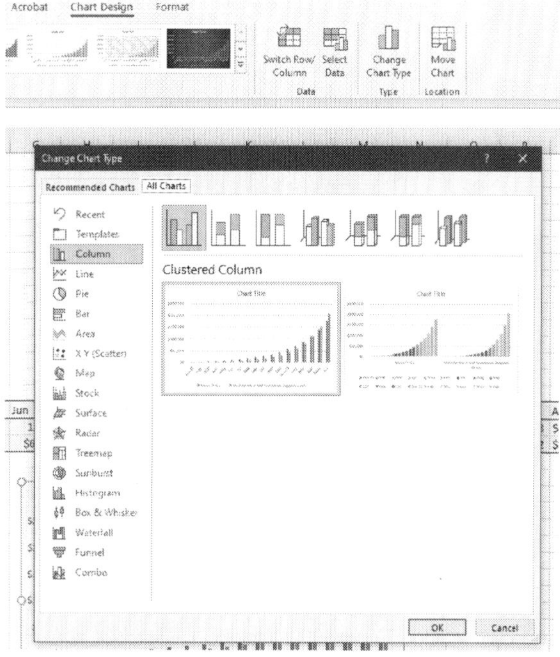

FIGURE 1.20

To add and customize data labels, titles, legend, or anything along these lines, simply use the “Add Chart Element” menu.

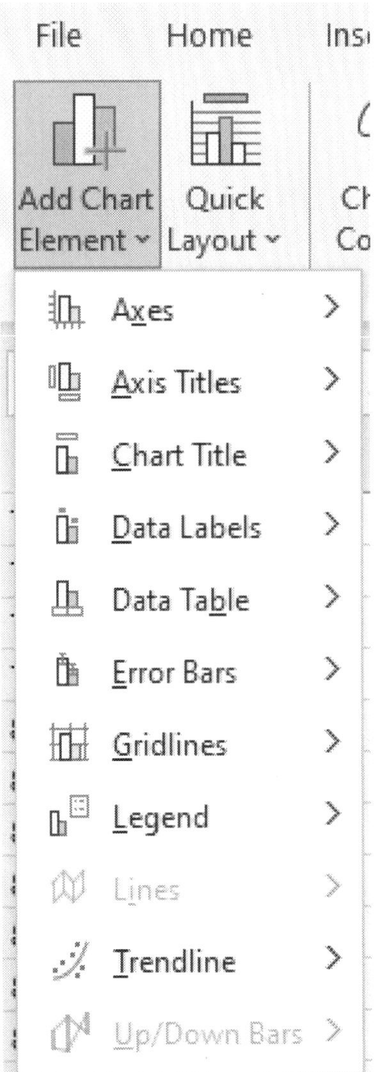

FIGURE 1.21

Double click on a specific chart element to open up the "format" menu. This allows you to customize the color, line weight, titles, and other details.

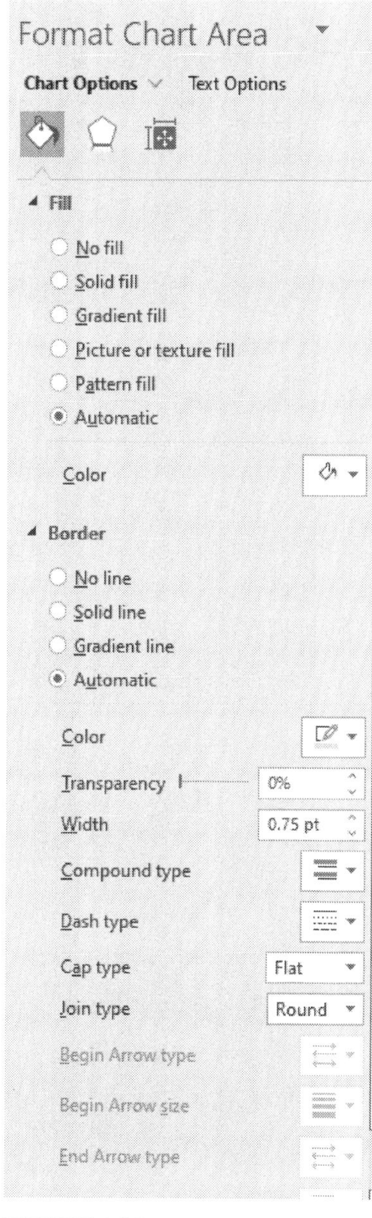

FIGURE 1.23

That was a very brief introduction to creating charts through excel, and I hope it gives you more clarity on creating awesome visuals. Go and experiment yourself and see what you can come up with!

- **Tableau**

Tableau is a data visualization tool that can visualize data and get a clear opinion based on the data analysis. It is the top dog for visualization tools and can turn data into a helpful visualization very efficiently. It is proficient in handling large and changing datasets due to its integration with some advanced database solutions, including Amazon AWS, My SQL, Hadoop, Teradata, and SAP. It also has a very high level of security.

- **Qlikview**

Qlikview is one of Tableau's top competitors. It is highly customizable and has a wide range of features. It can be a bit more of a learning curve to get a feel for it. It also offers powerful business analytics and intelligence reporting capabilities. Qlikview can be used alongside Qlik Sense which handles data exploration and discovery.

- **FusionCharts**

FusionCharts is a javascript-based charting tool. It can prudence about 90 different chart types, integrate with many platforms, and has a lot of flexibility. What makes Fusion-

Charts so attractive is that you can choose from many live templates and simply plug in your data sources.

It does not matter what tool you are using. What matters is that you follow the specific principles that allow your charts to be most effective when combined with the narrative of your data story. Therefore, I encourage you to explore and experiment with tools for chart creation to find the one that works best for you.

Now that we have gotten the basics of the visuals down, let's jump right into the next chapter, where we will define how you can refine your visuals for an even harder impact when presenting to your audience.

4
REFINING YOUR VISUALS - DEVELOPING A WINNING DESIGN

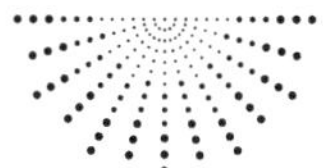

"You can achieve simplicity in the design of effective charts, graphs, and tables by remembering three fundamental principles: restrain, reduce, emphasize."

— *GARR REYNOLDS*

Having the right visualizations that enhance your narrative is a step in the right direction in hooking your audience before you even say a word. However, if these data visualizations aren't designed to appeal to the aesthetic this audience resonates with, all that effort beforehand would have been for nothing. Let's ensure that you are not wasting your time or your energy.

Always, and, I cannot stress this enough, always keep in mind that the data you are presenting is only as valuable as it is understandable to your audience. Deciding on the type of charts helpful in conveying your message is indeed an important one. Still, the work needs to be followed up, making it attractive and easy to digest mentally. With just one glance, you want to capture the attention of this audience. Remember how short the human attention span is currently. You need to make sure that this audience wants to learn more. Your aesthetic plays a vital role in developing that want. Therefore, while your chart might best represent the data, the audience can be pulled away from the message if the fonts interrupt the reading experiences, if the colors are too loud, or if the headings do not correspond with the delivered data.

With so many options when it comes to design, you can get caught up making the visual data pretty. But you must remember that the primary function of these visuals is to inform. The look must serve as a complement to that purpose. Even a visually unappealing chart that informs is better than a chart whose message gets lost in the quest to make the chart visually attractive.

Still, you want to hit your audience with a double whammy with charts that are both attractive and informative. You have taken care of the informative part with the development of the narrative and choosing the right type of charts. Next comes making decisions that make that data appealing to the eyes of the audience.

This part of this book focuses on how you can create clean and simple data visualizations that allow you to capture your audience's attention immediately. Only after you have hooked their attention can you deliver the key points precisely and with a resounding impact that increases the likelihood that your audience will be moved to act on your call-to-action. The winning design is free of clutter, has the proper use of color, is clean and precise, and is founded on design psychology. We will focus on each of these critical points and more now. Let's jump right in.

THE PSYCHOLOGY OF DESIGN

We have talked about visual perception and how it plays a part in how your audience perceives the data visualizations you deliver to them. Let's take a deeper look into how the brain relates what you see and how this plays a part in the success of your presentation.

There is a science as to why we find certain things visually appealing in comparison to others. That science extends to why your audience will be attracted to certain data visualizations instead of others, even when these charts display the same information.

Therefore, the first thing that needs to be addressed when developing a winning strategy for creating visuals that your audience wants to look at is not color schemes or font types. Instead, you need to delve into how humans mentally process images. Only then can you design and manipulate these mental pathways in your favor.

These mental pathways are known as artistic psychology. More precisely, it goes by the name of pre-attentive attributes. This is the process by which information catches a person's attention based on the visual images delivered to the brain so that the data delivered can be processed.

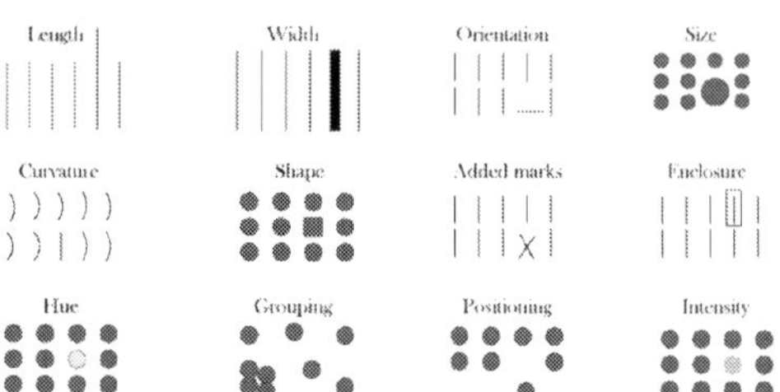

FIGURE 2- Pre-attentive attributes

Think of times that your eyes have been trained in a particular direction, but you do not remember a single time from that period of looking. This is because nothing during that time captures your attention visually. Therefore, the brain did not allocate resources to translate what that visual input might mean.

On the other hand, there are times when so much catches your attention visually that you do not know where to look next. That is pre-attentive attributes at work. That is the effect you want to stimulate when your audience looks at your graphs.

With the knowledge of pre-attentive attributes in your back pocket, you can design visuals that catch your audiences' attention. There are four qualities about an image that affect whether or not that image catches attention. These qualities are:

- Form
- Color
- Spatial position
- Movement

Let's take a look at what each of these elements means.

Movement refers to the use of flicker and motion elements related to images. A classic example of this is used in traffic lights. Banner ads also make frequent use of this element. These can, of course, be used in data visualizations; however, the use must be carefully weighed as it can be more distracting than aiding in capturing your audiences' attention. The audience may become captivated by the flickering effect rather than the information being relayed.

Spatial positioning speaks to the perception gained about an object's position relative to another object or one's self. It also refers to how a person might perceive that this object is turned relative to themselves. More specifically, does this person believe that the object is behind, in front of, left or right of, above, or below their person? 2D and 3D usage are examples of spatial positioning at work in data visualizations. The use of spatial positioning apart from 2D positioning can add depth to your data visualizations. Still, the use is not typically recommended because, just like flicker and motions usage, they can detract from the message rather than enhance it.

We will discuss color more in-depth later in this chapter. Let's take a deeper look at the element of form now.

Form refers to the structure of the elements that make up your visualizations. Therefore, this takes into account things like:

- Length
- Width
- Orientation
- Size
- Curvature
- Shape

- Added marks
- Enclosure
- Hue
- Grouping
- Positioning
- Intensity

...and more in relation to your chart. For example, the form would refer to the bars' height, width, degree of curvature, and hue in a bar chart. The wonderful thing about form is that it can help attract attention to certain parts of your data visualizations while detracting attention from other parts.

On the other hand, the improper use of form can make an element distracting. For example, if the tops of the bars in your bar charts are curved instead of straight, the audience may spend more time determining the actual value being represented instead of the connections you are trying to convey. You want to make it easy for your audience to extract information from your chart and move on swiftly. This will significantly increase your engagement and the incidence of the audience members being moved to the call-to-action.

The form also allows for creating uniformity in your charts. This makes for a straightforward interpretation of data as well as differentiation of differing elements. For example, each unit of a pie chart represents a certain percentage or fraction of the whole and allows for easier interpretation of the proportions of data being presented. Likewise, the height of each bar on a bar chart allows for that data to be mentally digested.

All of the qualities that contribute to the pre-attentive mental process do not happen on a conscious level. They are not things that you have to think that you have to process for them to happen. They just do, and it only takes fractions of milliseconds for human attention to be captured by such elements. Let's have a look at how we can use these to our advantage. As you can see in this horizontal bar chart there is valuable information, but someone seeing this chart for the first time won't necessarily understand the significance of it.

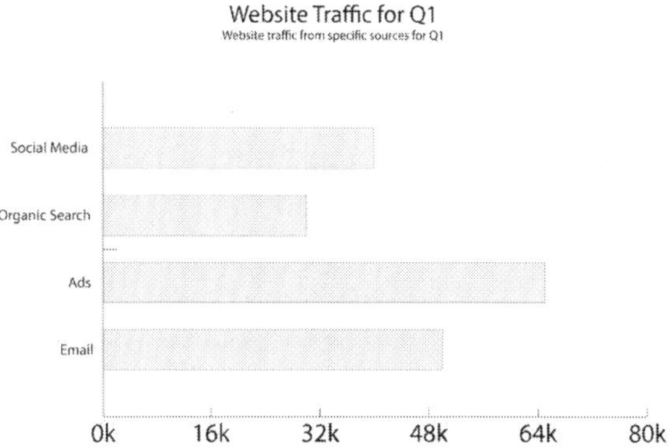

FIGURE 2.1 Not very memorable - Charted values with no known significance.

Rearranging the bars and highlighting specific information in green will better get your point across.

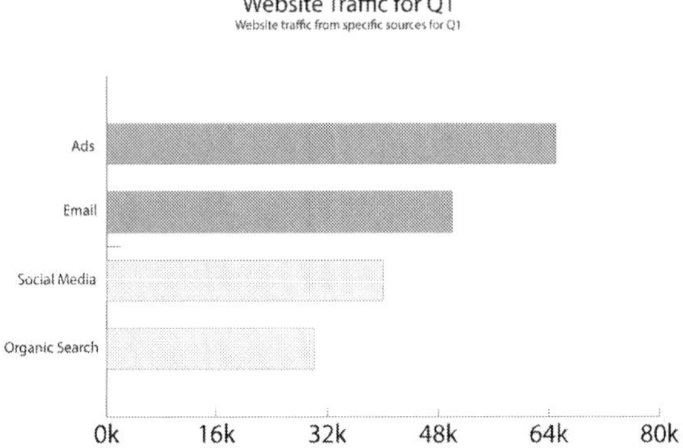

FIGURE 2.2 Use attributes to your advantage - Highlighting best performing sources in green to better understand the data. (Green tends to be a color representing something that is good)

The same can be done if you want to showcase the areas that didn't perform as well as expected.

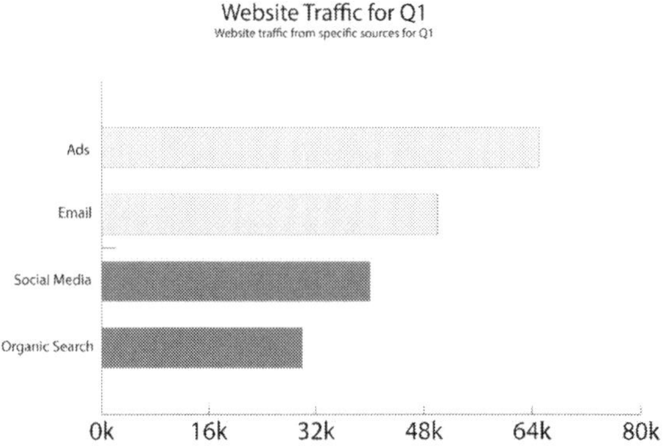

FIGURE 2.3 Using color to draw attention to specific values. (Use a color like red or yellow, these colors normally indicate something negative or slow.)

Adequately incorporating these elements into your data visualizations gets your audience's subconscious mind on board with the message you are trying to convey... once you do it the right way. Once performed well, though, incorporating these elements into the design of your data story allows for seamless interpretation of even the most complex data.

Let's go back to the previous scenario we used in chapter 2 and have a look at another example.

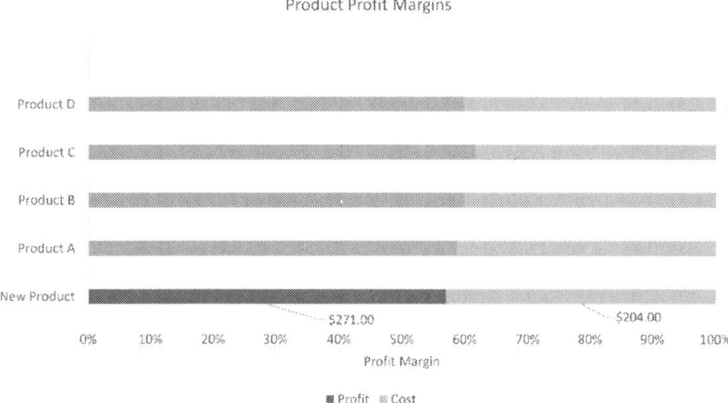

FIGURE 2.4 Highlighting specific information like profit, cost, so it is easily distinguishable from the rest.

Although the other products' information is important, it is not what the audience wants. By initially showing them all of the products, then honing in on our main focus, they can easily distinguish the valuable information from the supporting information. We used similar tactics in the next visual.

FIGURE 2.5 Utilizing color and text to signify our points.

As you see here, we want the competitors' data to support our validity, not undermine it. Adding our initial and recommended price point while showcasing the price range in a separate color emphasizes our point while showing the relevance to the competitors. Adding the "AVG" competitor price also helps reassure the reasoning for our price point.

At a glance, the audience can view all the valuable information without confusion.

The Gestalt Principles of Perception

Something worth familiarizing yourself with is the Gestalt Principles of Perception. At the Gestalt School of Psychology, they observed that humans naturally organize things in particular ways to try and make sense of it. The Gestalt theory emphasizes that the whole of anything is more significant than its parts. The theory consists of several principles that describe how we perceive visual information. They are:

Proximity: Objects close together are perceived as a group.

Proximity

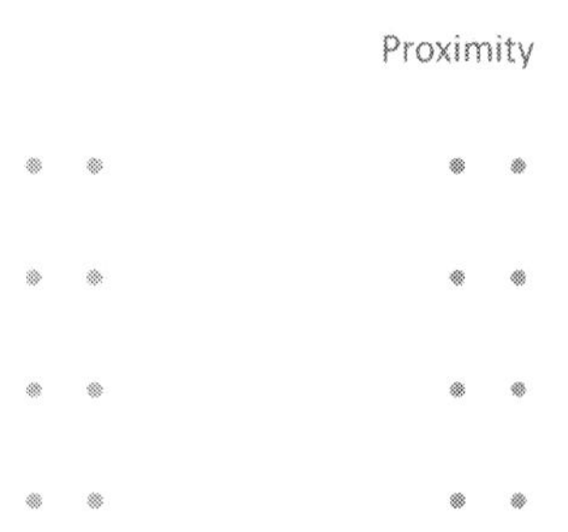

FIGURE 2.6

Continuation: Objects that are aligned or in continuation of one and another are perceived as a group.

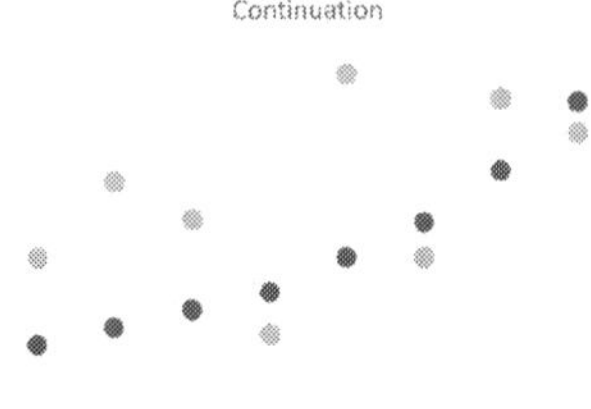

FIGURE 2.7

Similarity: Objects that share similar details such as color or shape are perceived as a group.

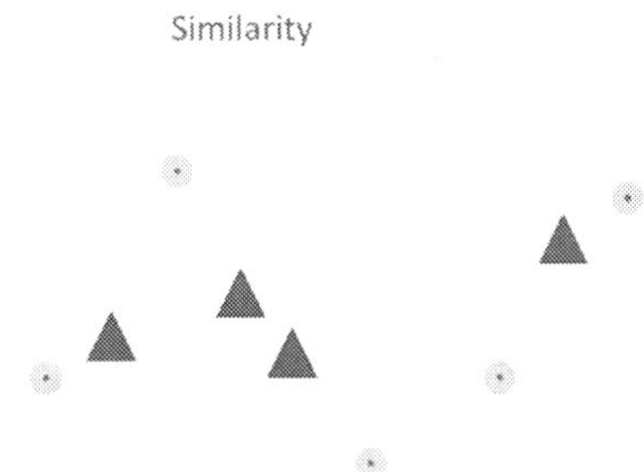

FIGURE 2.8

Connection: Objects connected (e.g., by a line) are perceived as a group.

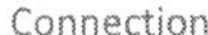

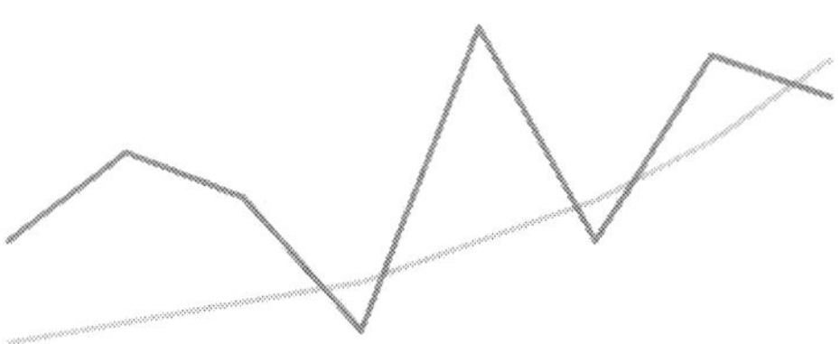

FIGURE 2.9

Enclosure: Objects that have some sort of boundary enclosing them are perceived as a group.

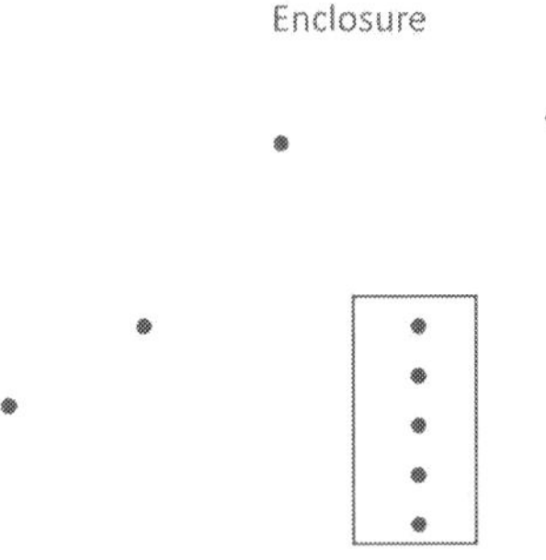

FIGURE 2.10

Closure: Our mind tends to add missing pieces of familiar shapes. When we are faced with objects that seem to be incomplete or open, we tend to perceive them as closed and complete. .(e.g., why a graph only needs an X and Y axis.)

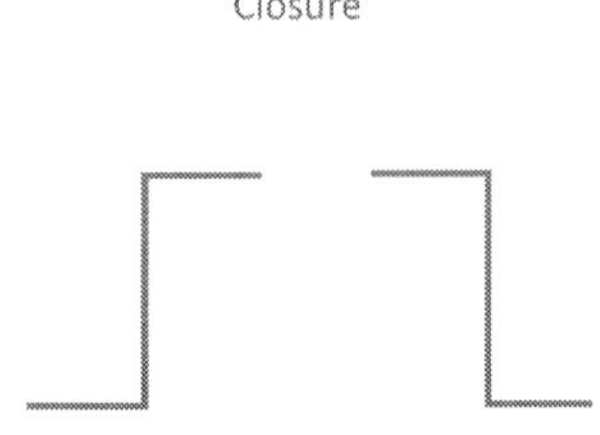

FIGURE 2.11

The true purpose behind the Gestalt Principles is to understand how we perceive information. When applied correctly, we can deliver the information to our audience in the most effective way possible. Keep these principles in mind when creating data visualizations. Use these principles to highlight key insights in your visualizations.

COMMON MISTAKES MADE WHEN CREATING DATA VISUALIZATIONS

Often to get a good picture of how you should perform a task correctly, you need to know how *not* to perform that task. There are a few data visualizations mistakes that are common among business professionals. These mistakes can be off-putting to the audience and leave them with a bad taste in their mouth about that presentation. It might even leave them questioning the ethics of that analyst.

However, typically the data analyst does not make those mistakes out of malicious or destructive intent. They are simply honest mistakes born out of ignorance. You may find that even you have been guilty of making these same mistakes when utilizing data visualizations. If you are indeed guilty, note that this is not the end of the world, especially now that you are on a path to knowing better.

To set you on the right path, we will go over some of the top mistakes made when designing visualizations, how you can spot them, and how you can correct them.

Misleading Color Contrast

Color can add that special panache that your visuals need to convey accurate and adequate amounts of information to your audience when used correctly. The improper use of that color can lead to your audience being confused and deceived about what you are trying to convey with the information that you are presenting.

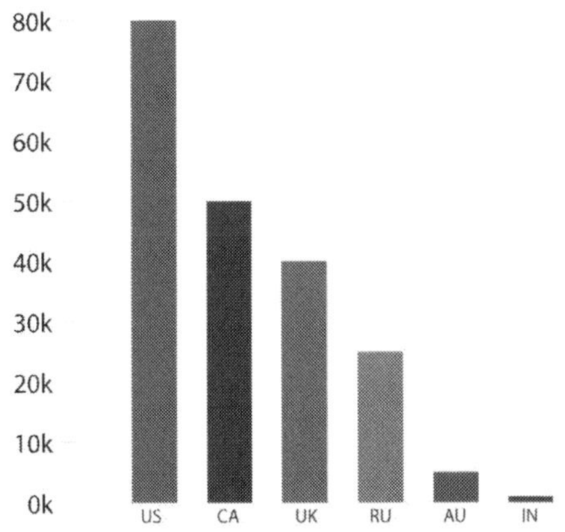

FIGURE 2.12 Unnecessary color - The use of color in this graph has no significance and may have your audience drawing conclusions that aren't warranted.

I chose to print the book in B+W to keep print costs down to ensure the book was as affordable as possible. If you would like the full-color PDF to view the visualizations as intended, sign up at ElizabethSClarke.com and respond to the first email. I will happily send you the full-color version. Thank you for your patience.

Color is not just used for purely aesthetic reasons, even though it can be pleasing to the eye. It is a persuasive element that shows degrees of contrast so that your audience notes disparities and differences in the information presented. If highlighting differences in values isn't necessary, avoid adding unnecessary colors.

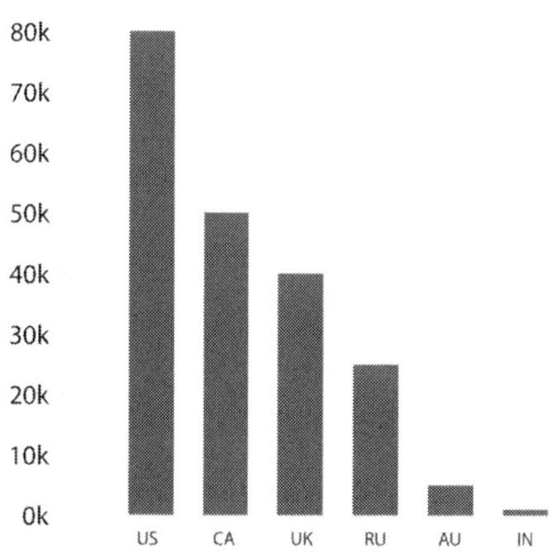

FIUGRE 2.13 Using color effectively - Keeping colors uniform and ordering graph appropriately will warrant a clear understanding of the data.

Highly contrasting color elements can cause the audience to believe that there is a greater degree of disparity than there really is. Therefore, it is best to use similar colors such as different shades of the same color for highlighting information with similarities and use higher levels of contrast like two completely different colors to show differences in the data presented.

Improper Use of 3D Graphics

Many data analysts are trying to adopt 3D data modeling but simply are not using it correctly. You should only use a 3D chart when a third dimension must be highlighted in your data story. While these graphics add visual interest, they do not always benefit the presentation. While data 3D graphics can be engaging, they can lead to confusion about the scale of differences and similarities between different datasets. They can also possibly obstruct how the audience perceives this data.

There is a simple way to avoid this potential mishap occurring in your presentation. Simply do not use 3D graphics unless there is a very good reason for doing so, which is the addition of dimensions that merely cannot be expressed effectively in 2D. The use of traditional 2D graphics eliminates these problems. The age-old saying of *don't fix it if it ain't broke* applies here.

Too Much Data

With so many bytes of data being produced about a business every single day, it can be challenging to determine what needs to be included in your presentations and visualizations and what does not need to be included. Being so close to your data, you may feel that every single byte of information is crucial to share to tell the entire story. However, too much information will simply overwhelm your audience. This overload of information makes the members of your audience zone out away from what you are trying to convey. This leads to less engagement and your call to action not being acted on.

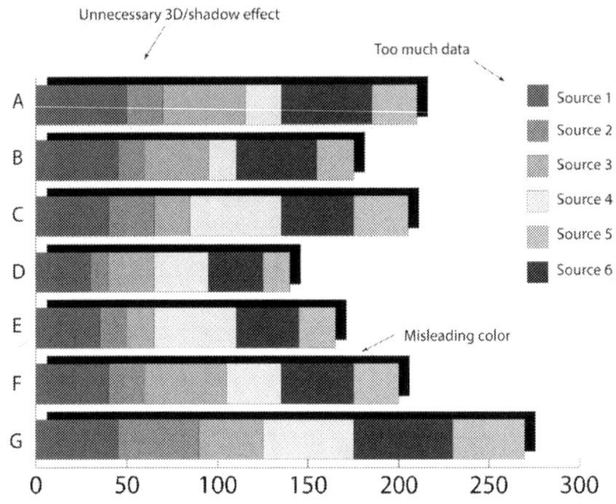

FIGURE 2.14 Too much data means clutter - Cluttering your graph with data and unnecessary elements will lead to confusion. Every element including the data must add significance to the graph so the viewer can easily understand what it is conveying.

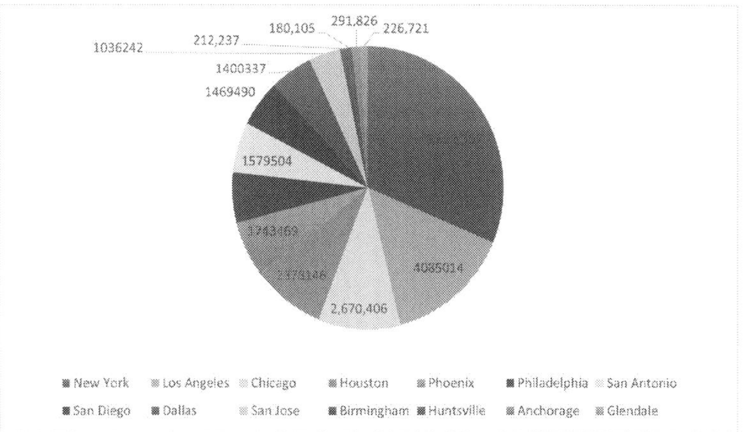

FIGURE 2.15 Another example of too much data.

The solution is to keep things as simple as possible. This means condensing the data into a limited number of visualizations or using multiple visualizations at different points in your presentation to present the audience with easier-to-digest information in smaller quantities. Lets have a look at another example:

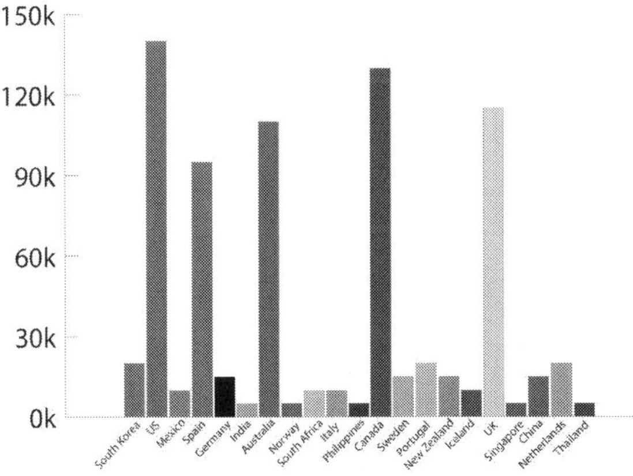

FIGURE 2.16 Overwhelming data - having too much data with no specific meaning will be confusing to most audiences.

When dealing with a data set similar to this one, try simplifying the data. Showcase the top five sets of values and mark the rest as "other". If your audience is needing more information about the "other" values you can create a few extra charts showcasing each specific point.

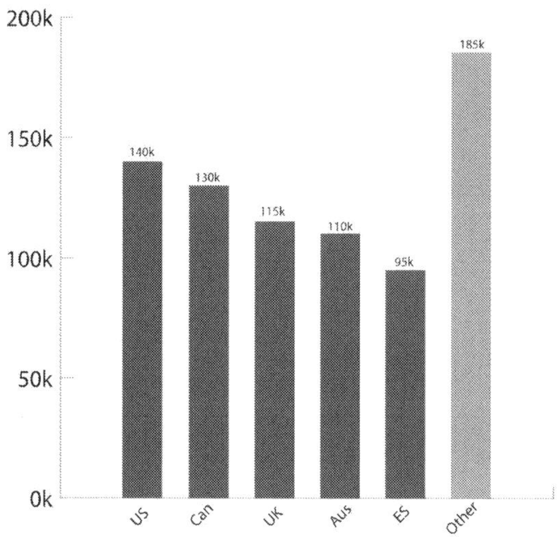

FIGURE 2.17 Simplifying the data - Simplify the data by showcasing the top five values in order. Expand upon any specific points or values if needed.

Omitting Baselines and Truncating Scale

To make data more digestible to the audience, some analysts choose to manipulate scales on charts. An example of this in action is to omit the baseline or start somewhere above the zero mark on the chart's Y-axis. This is typically done to make the differences in data more noticeable. Another example of this in action is replacing or shortening the X-axis value in datasets to be more comparable to lower values in that dataset.

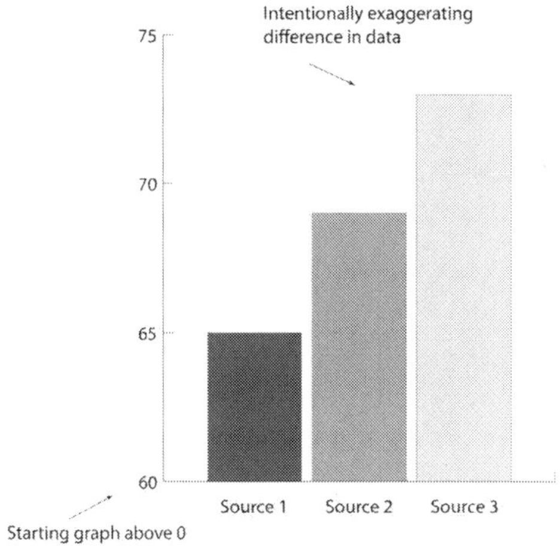

FIGURE 2.18 Starting graph above zero - Misleading your audience with an exaggerated scale may have viewers drawing conclusions that are inaccurate.

While these practices can indeed make it easier for some audiences to digest the data, they can also make it confusing and misleading to most. Essentially, these practices exaggerate or minimize the differences in datasets, which is unethical when presenting data to an audience. The solution here? Simply do not incorporate these practices in your data visualizations. Make sure to keep your visuals accurate and clear.

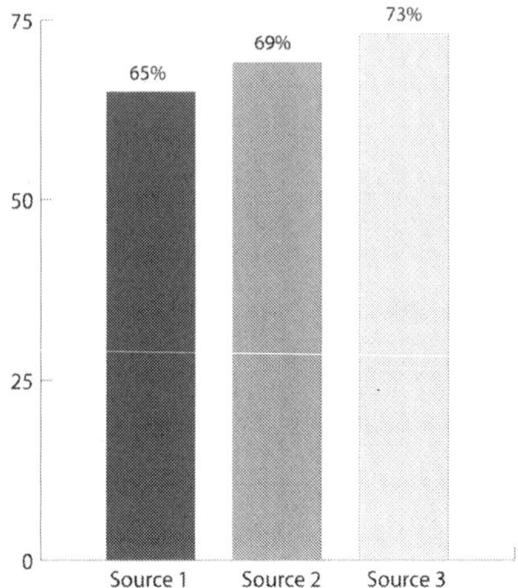

FIGURE 2.19 Proper scale - Compared to figure 2.17, you can see the values are closer to one another and do not warrant any serious action that figure 2.17 might have hinted to.

Choosing the Wrong Visualization Method

Choosing the right charts to support your presentation is not a game of eeny, meeny, miny, moe. There is an art and a science to this because data visualizations are not one size fits all. For example, using bar charts can make differences and similarities between different datasets more apparent. In contrast, when doing a simple parts of a whole analysis a pie chart might be well suited as long as you can easily distinguish the values.

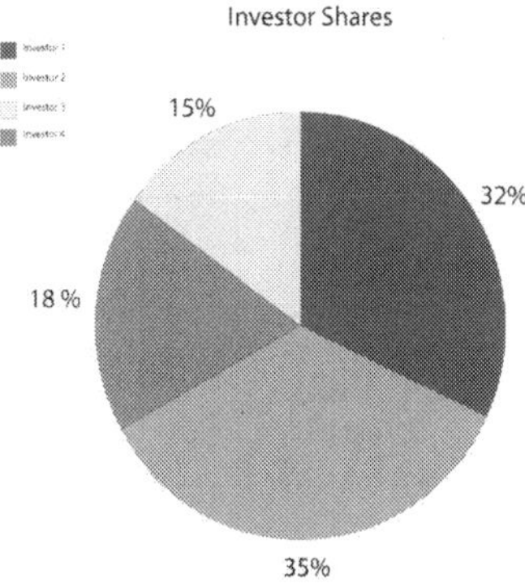

FIGURE 2.20 Not the best choice for this particular set of data. Your graph should enhance the meaning of the data, not make it more confusing.

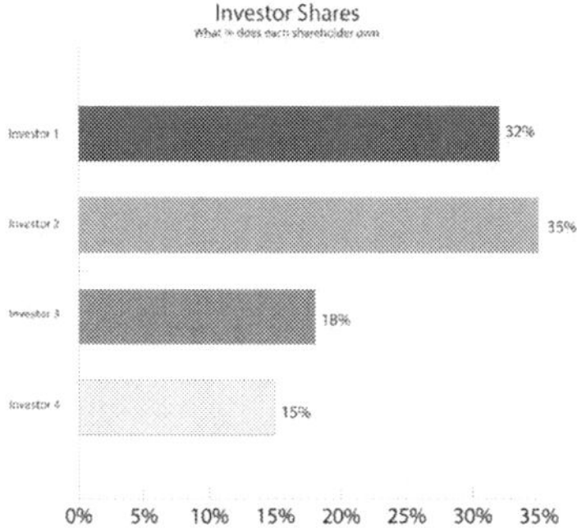

Figure 2.21 A better graph for this particular set of data.

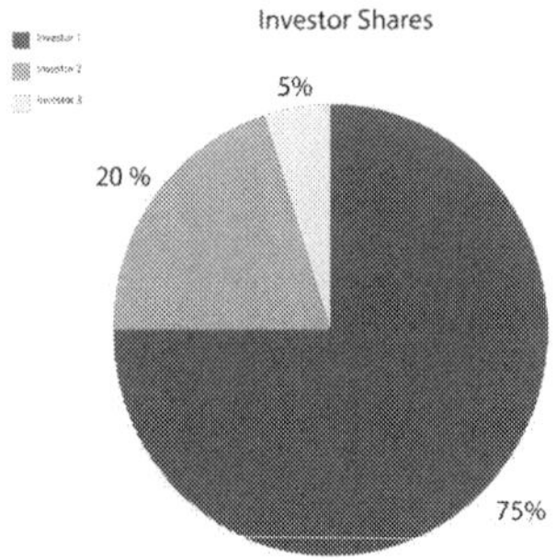

FIGURE 2.22 Using the proper chart allows for better interpretation of the data at first glance.

The type of data visualization you choose can get your audience on board with what you are trying to convey or make them more confused at first glance.

Avoiding that problem by taking the time to understand what your visuals must convey and then choosing the right charts to correlate with that ultimate vision.

Confusing Correlations

Using visuals to show correlations between different datasets is a helpful way of giving your audience a broader understanding of the data being presented. One of the best ways to show correlations is to overlay them in the same chart. However, having too many different datasets highlighted in one chart can lead to confusion. Instead of showing connections and inciting an "*aha*" moment, it can lead to the opposite effect, which is the "*huh?*" Moment. Too many data analysts try to use correlations to show the cause of what drives that data to be what it is. This will always fail because correlation is not synonymous with cause.

Instead of using what can be an unethical practice, it is better to use multiple visualizations to show how different datasets can be connected rather than overlaying them in a single chart. These multiple visualizations can still allow for that "*aha*" moment when the audience connects the relationships between different datasets.

Biased Text Descriptions

The inclusion of text is also part of designing your data visualizations. Just like everything else in the design process, the text needs to be considered carefully. All texts such as titles, captions, and labels need to support and provide an unbiased view of the data displayed in your charts. These texts are part of what persuades your audience to perform your call to action.

However, the problem lies in the fact that some business professionals use this text to manipulate how the audience perceives the data. This practice creates a bias towards a certain opinion or view. This is an unethical practice. Let's say you're visualizing The sales figures from Q1, showing a steady growth month over month. However, with this growth has come extra business costs, leaving profits smaller as revenue increases. Ignoring this important information may help you look good in the short term but will be detrimental in the long term. Our goal is to improve future trends and solve problems, not hide them. Don't focus solely on the good data. The bad can be just as important.

Cherry-picking Data

Cherry-picking data is when an analyst may only visualize specific data points to better support their narrative while leaving out crucial, contradictory evidence. For example, if sales are steady throughout Quarters 1-3, then dives Q4, they may only present quarters 1-3, claiming they are on a steady growth trajectory. In reality, the marketing methods working for them might need some adjusting due to the downturn.

DECLUTTERING YOUR DATA VISUALIZATIONS

Think about it. If you walk into a room with furniture, trash, all sorts of miss-matched pieces everywhere, you will be confused about what you should look at and how you should act in that room. This causes mental confusion. Most people are not able to be productive in a space that is cluttered like this.

The same analogy applies to your data visualizations. Data visualizations that are cluttered cause mental confusion, so your audience will not know where to look first or next. All that mental noise will cause most people to zone out and become less engaged with your presentation. Avoided that mental confusion by applying the apt saying, *less is more.*

Two different charts presenting the same data can have vastly different reactions because of the amount of information placed and how it is placed. Obviously, you want to be on the side of the fence where you present a good chart that is aesthetically pleasing and gives context to your audience. Lets look at a bad example, then figure out what we can do to redesign it:

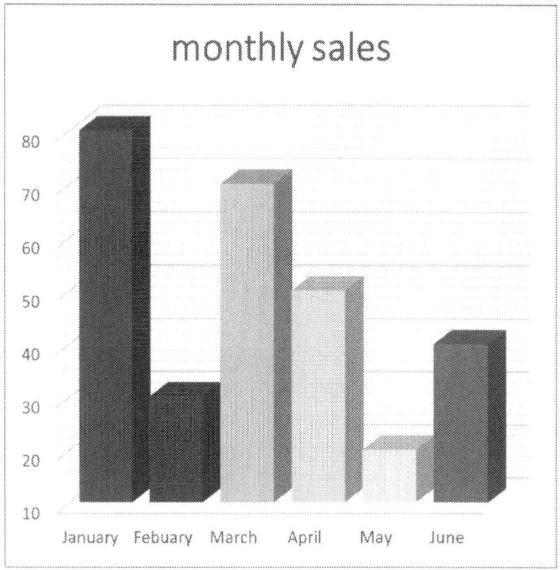

FIGURE 2.23 Example of a chart that needs a redesign

Start Your Bar Chart at Zero (0)

Think of the X and Y axis of your charts as the skeleton. Things will be skewed if you are missing bones from that skeleton. Zero is part of the makeup of the skeleton, and removing it will skew the look of that chart. Starting your chart above zero makes the bars of your chart misleading, and this skewed view will confuse your audience, and you would be representing the data inaccurately.

Ensure you have a "proper" decluttered chart by starting the origin as zero. Follow that up with ensuring that your axes are evenly scaled, placing uniformed spaces between the bars, and placing the bars in chronological order or in order of size.

Remove the Chart Border

Chart borders do not add information value to your visualizations. Often it is visually more appealing to watch white space rather than the clutter that these elements add.

Column Etiquette

As mentioned before, 3D charts can obstruct information and be misleading if they do not serve a very specific function. In addition, they can make charts harder to read and add clutter that is unnecessary to the presentation. 2D graphics are typically more suitable for effective data storytelling. Also, we should always take column width into account. Wide columns take away from the smooth visual flow we are going for. Consider medium/thinner stacks. Trust your judgment.

Steer Away from Dark Gridlines

Your charts need to be simple enough that the audience can note from a single glance what is being presented along each axis of your chart. Therefore, the need for gridlines should be zero or minimal.

The best practice is to eliminate the use of gridlines as they add unnecessary noise. In cases where they are necessary, use soft, grey gridlines instead of harsh, black gridlines.

Avoid Overuse of Bright, Bold Colors

Colors should be used to show similarities and differences and to provide context to your data story. Just as you should not use high color contrast to avoid misleading the audience, you need to also limit the amount of color you use. Bold, bright colors pull attention in several directions at once and make it hard to concentrate on specific elements of data visualizations.

Proper Use of Text

Ensure that the title properly describes the information given in the chart, and has the proper title case. The X and Y axis should be readable and easily understood. We will look deeper into text at the end of the chapter.

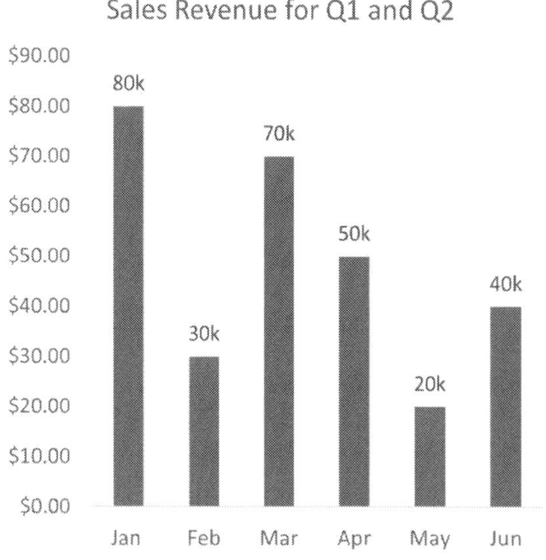

Figure 2.24 What it should look like - Bar graph with proper scale and removal of distracting elements such as gridlines, chart border, and unnecessary color. Clear and Descriptive title.

The best practice for using color is to use a single color and vary the shades to show similarities and differences or use a spectrum between two similar colors to show a range of data.

Let's walk through a full chart redesign together. How about we use our chart from chapter 2 and see how we got it to that point. This is where we started off after turning our data into an excel auto-populated chart. (You can do this by highlighting your data and selecting ALT-F1)

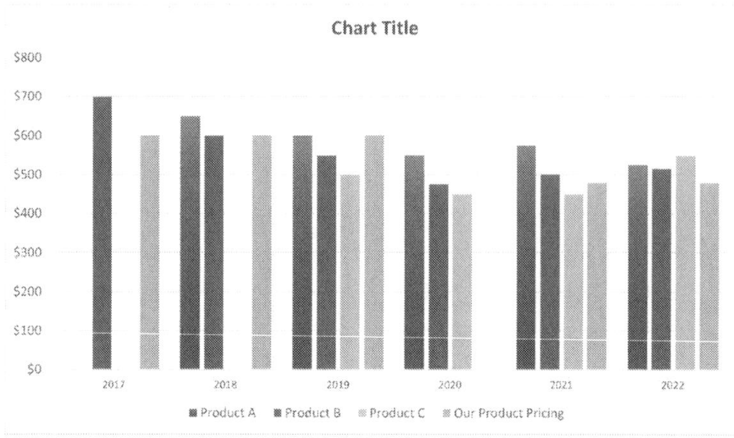

FIGURE 2.25 Confusing bar chart.

The first thing to decide is chart type. What would be best for this scenario? As you can see with the bar graph, It doesn't visually represent the data effectively. It's hard to distinguish the average price point without someone telling you what it is. We don't want that. Our main goal is for the audience to make the right conclusions independently through an effective visualization.

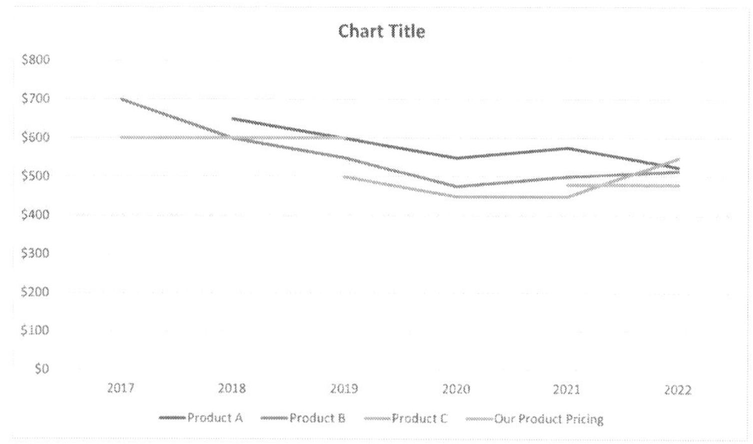

FIGURE 2.26 Line chart is better for recording trajectory over time.

A line graph is a lot more effective for this type of data as you can see determine the average without any information about it. There's still a lot to do before it becomes presentable.

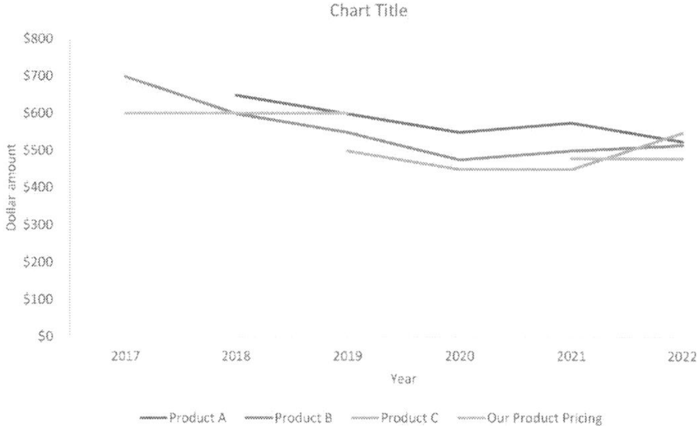

FIGURE 2.27 Adjusting text and lines

Let's start with the text and lines. A more subtle title and removal of gridlines looks very clean for this specific chart. I also removed the chart border to keep the visual flow. The legend has a few extra unnecessary elements, but we will get back to that. Let's do our axis labels. I kept it simple with "Dollar amount" and "Year" in this case.

That's all they need to know in terms of axis labels. The title is a bit more critical. Keeping it simple yet effective is what we should strive for.

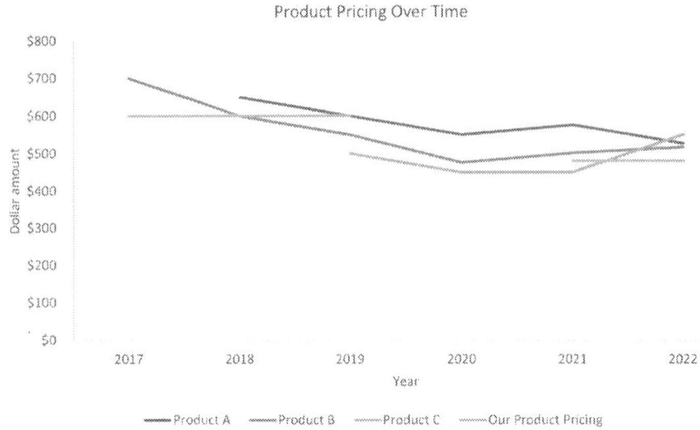

FIGURE 2.28

What exactly are we showing our audience? We shouldn't complicate it. In this scenario, "product pricing over time" should do the trick. We don't want them humming and hawing trying to understand the title and what's being presented to them. We want their eyes to go right to the relevant information available in the visual.

Let's address the color and legend. In this case, the competitors add valuable supporting information, to show the average product price and where we should be in relation. They don't need to be the star of the show. Let's make them all neutral and make our product something easy to see, and pleasant on the eyes. Let's also change the legend to be "competitors" to categorize them as one.

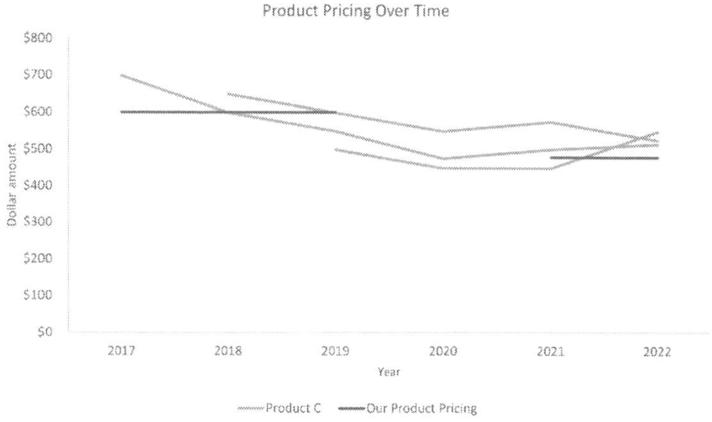

FIGURE 2.29

Now I THINK it's time to add some attributes to emphasize the main points. What exactly needs to be showcased?

1. What each line represents(Products)
2. What our initial price range was, what our new price range is, and why we changed it.
3. What the new average product price point is (so it's relatable to our price).

Let's add these. If you're using excel, these are called "Data Labels" and can be added by right-clicking middle of chart > Add data labels. Simply remove, reposition, and edit them as desired.

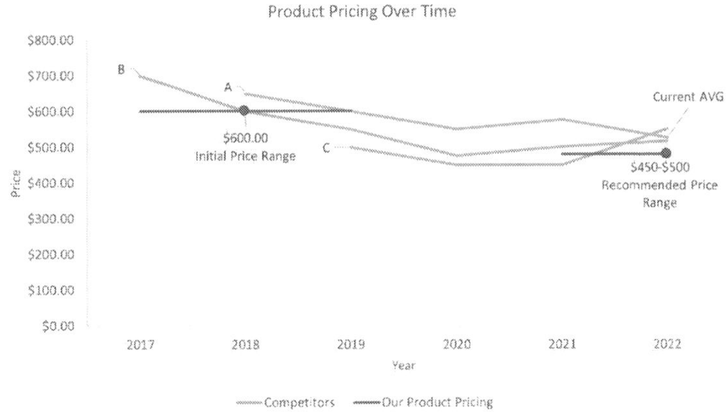

FIGURE 2.30

Here we have added our initial price point, the competitor average, and the new price point in relation to the competitors. Right away, you can see we are just below the competitors to remain competitive. Pair this with the "Product Profit Margins" chart from chapter 2, and you can easily show that we are the most competitive option while hitting our target for profitability.

Use the tips above to create charts that quiet the noise and steer your audience to the message you convey. Loud, cluttered charts tend to push audiences away rather than draw them in, but your data visualizations will be a lot more impactful if you apply the above principles to create clean concise charts.

Here is a quick tip if you are having trouble designing charts that stun - visit ElizabethSClarke.com or scan the QR and download my free data visualization checklist. This tool can be a game changer for new data analysts as you can adequately assess your charts to make sure all the elements are correctly executed and set up for success. Its absolutely free and a lot better than memorizing this whole section!

THE COLOR EXPERIENCE

A compelling data story is memorable and easy to digest. The same can be said about effective data visualization. Color is one element that makes it easier to achieve that memorability and easy digestion of information.

However, while color can add depth and dimension to your data visualization, it can also distract your audience from the information you were trying to convey. Unfortunately, most data storytellers have a distracted audience because of the improper use of color when designing data visualizations. That poor association is often the result of not understanding color theory and how to use color palettes when creating aesthetically pleasing yet informative visuals. You cannot just throw colors together and hope for the best. You have to be strategic about how, why, and when you use them.

We have touched on several aspects of color theory above. It is time to dive into how you can choose a color palette that compliments the intentions of your visualizations rather than distracts from it. While you can, of course, stick to one color in your charts, using a limited range of colors can add something unique to the same information. This range of colors is your color palette.

This range is not thrown together randomly, though, if you want that color to be effective. There are three color palette types that you can fall back on to make your charts pop in a good way, even if you do not have a design bone in your body. These types are:

Qualitative Palettes

With such a color palette, the colors used are distinctive. For example, if four colors are used in a line chart, they may be green, purple, orange, and yellow. Qualitative palettes are typically used when the variables are categorical and clearly different. For example, a line chart may be designed to show the unemployment rate in different countries over five years. Each line would represent a different country, which is a different category. This is distinct, and so each line would be colored differently.

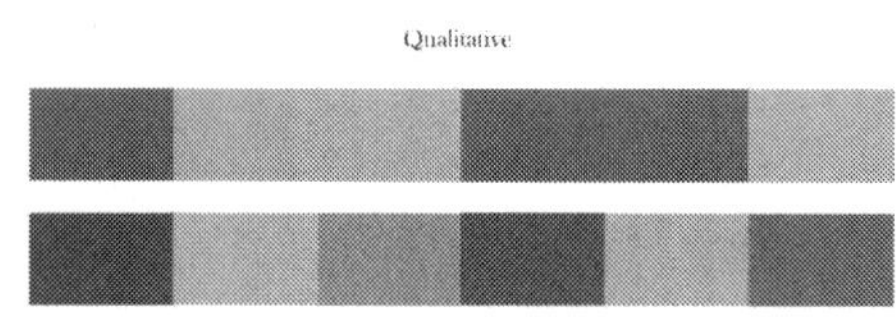

FIGURE 2.31 Qualitative color palette.

When using a qualitative color palette to design your chart, you may be tempted to go buck wild with the color input, but this is a temptation that you need to resist. Ideally, you should limit the number of colors used to 6. On the far end, you may go up to 10 colors but no further. The use of too many colors brings up the audience's inability to distinguish between the colors used as the chart becomes cluttered. This leaves far too much room for misinterpretation. If you find that your categories exceed ten total, the alternative is to bundle similar categories together or bundle categories with smaller values together and label this as "other."

Here are a few rules to stick by when using a qualitative color palette to design your charts:

- Ensure that the colors are used to complement each other so that the chart remains visually appealing.
- Ensure that different categories are distinct by ensuring different colors are used. This can be done by adjusting color saturation and lightness.
- Ensure that the color differences are not too significant, as this can lead the audience into thinking that some categories carry more importance than others.
- Do not use the same colors more than once, unless the categories have a relationship of some kind and a similar hue can be used.

Sequential Palettes

This type of color palette makes use of color by adding variations with different saturation. For example, there may be six variations that need to be presented on a chart. The color used on this chart to show these data variations is pink. Each of these variations will have its value represented by a different shade of pink.

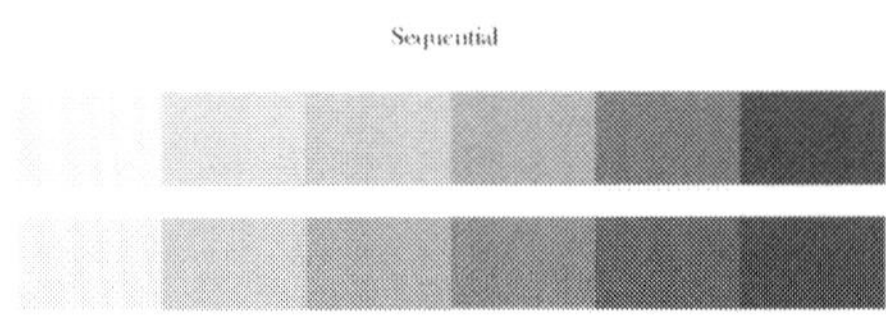

FIGURE 2.32 Sequential color palette.

Sequential color palettes are typically used when the variable values are numeric or ordered. For example, a chart showing wage changes in different companies over the four quarters of a year may be designed with a sequential palette. On the other hand, a diagram showing the percentage variables of a whole may also use a sequential palette.

Here are a few tips for gaining the most value when using a sequential color palette when designing your charts:

- Use lighter colors to depict lower values and darker shades to depict higher values when your chart is plotted on a white or light-colored background. Plot the variations from lighter to darker.
- Use darker colors to depict lower values and lighter colors to depict higher values when your chart is plotted on a dark background. Plot the variations from darker to lighter.
- More than one color may be used as well. This is done by also playing with the saturation of the colors used. For example, a chart may show the increasing temperature in a region by designing a chart that moves from a color hue like shades of blue to a

warmer hue like shades of yellow and, finally, a hotter hue like shades red.

- The visual designer can use a discrete or continuous color gradient when plotting the values with this color palette. A discrete palette is one where there is a clear distinction between the color saturations. Discrete color palettes may even make use of text-like number values to highlight that distinction. On the other hand, with continuous palettes, the saturation appears to merge into each other. The use of either type of palette is dependent on the goal of the visual designer. A discrete palette helps the audience easily digest the data. So, this is great for times when there is a greater range of data. Discrete palettes are also great for use when the variable ranges are vastly unequal in size. Continuous palettes are better when the varying ranges are relatively equal in size and when the range of data is shorter.

Diverging Palettes

When plotting variables with a central value like zero, divergent palettes are typically the go-to color palette. Two different sequential palettes are combined to show the movement of values. Values on either side of that central value are assigned a different color gradient. One of the most common situations where divergent color palettes are used is when negative and positive values are highlighted in one chart. The same rules for designing when using a sequential palette apply when creating charts with diverging palettes.

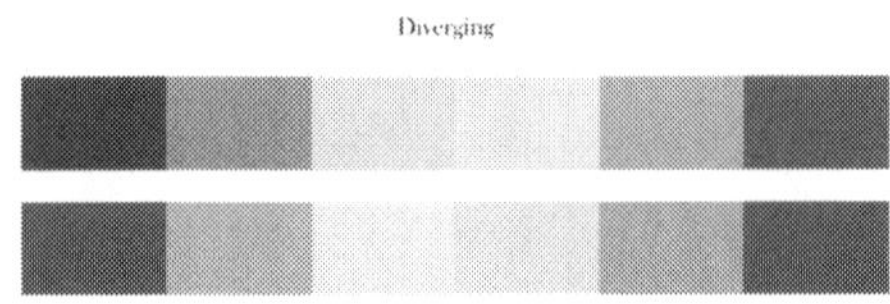

FIGURE 2.33 Diverging color palette.

The data color picker by Learn UI Design is an excellent tool to help you pick sequential and diverging palettes. Check it out here: https://learnui.design/tools/data-color-picker.html

BEST PRACTICES WHEN USING COLOR

In addition to keeping in mind the type of palette you use, here are a few tips for ensuring that your charts remain visually appealing to your audience.

Use Colors to Create Associations

Human beings have particular associations with color. For example, we see red and think stop or danger. Likewise, green is typically associated with nature and safety. These color associations invoke certain emotions within us. You can use these associations when designing your data visual to your advantage. Keep such associations in mind when you pick color palettes. For example, you may be presenting a data story to people from a certain university. When designing your visualizations, using their university flag colors can immediately invoke camaraderie in the audience and make them more receptive to your message.

Use a Single Color to Show Continuous Data

In situations where it is not permitted that your audience knows exact figures but rather that they recognize a trend, the use of continuous sequential and diverging palettes may be best. This allows the audience to grasp the trend quickly, whether increasing, decreasing, or unchanging so that you can link other information to that movement.

Use Contrasting Colors to Show Comparison and Contrast

Help your audience easily distinguish between datasets that are different with the use of different colors. For example, a social media analysis can easily distinguish the conversion rate of using organic traffic versus ads on Facebook with the help of the metrics being colored green and blue. On the other hand, if both metrics were colored the same, it would be harder to determine this at a single glance.

Use Color to Highlight Important Information

If you want your audience to focus on a particular piece of information, use a brighter color or a higher saturation of the single color used for that data set. This makes the information stand out from the rest. You can also choose to only color that set of information and leave the rest, less pertinent information, colored grey.

Do Not Pick Colors that Easily Merge Into Each Other

Once your audience starts to squint at your chart, you have failed to make the information easy to interpret with a glance. Avoid this situation by making the colors used when designing your chart easy to distinguish from each other. For example, if you are designing a line chart, using different shades of one color will incite that squinting effect. On the other hand, using a qualitative palette will allow for easier interpretation of the separate data trends with one look.

Keep Your Color Count at a Minimum

The colors of the rainbow are at your disposal when you design your charts. That does not mean that you should pick every color to infuse into your chart design. Make the colors relevant and also keep the color count down to avoid clutter. The maximum number of colors used should be kept at six. Any more and you risk your audience becoming overwhelmed and unable to interpret the information easily. If necessary, try and separate the data into two visuals.

Account for Accessibility

Color vision deficiencies are more prominent than most people realize. Some people can distinguish between separate colors. For example, orange and purple may look the same to some people. This is called color blindness. It is more common than you would think. Approximately once in twelve men are color blind. As a data storyteller, you need to account that some of your audience may suffer from such difficulties, and you need to cater to them as well. Be sure to research whether anyone in your audience faces visual challenges so that you can factor that into the development of your color palette. Sometimes, this information is not easy to source, so consider simply just designing every chart with this in mind.

THE PROPER USE OF TEXT

A problem that many new analysts run into is that they feel the need to explain every part of the data visualizations with the inclusion of excessive amounts of text. The thing that you do not realize to avoid repeating this mistake is that the data visualizations need to be strong enough to speak for themselves with a minimal amount of text.

When text is included, it needs to be done in a clean, concise manner that does not include lengthy paragraphs or unnecessary descriptions. Compelling text usually only consists of the labeling of axes if required and memorable, effective titles.

In keeping with the element of text inclusion, be sure to use a font that is appropriate for the presentation style and visualizations that you have chosen. If the font style and overall feel of the data presented do not mesh well, the audience will be put off from that experience.

While you should keep the use of text to a minimum in your data visualization, there is no denying that text does play an essential role in conveying the right message to your audience. Common text elements in data visualizations include captions, labels, titles, legends, and labeled icons. Despite their scarce use, the proper implementation of text in your data visualizations is a must. Lets look at a bad example of text, and what we can do to improve it.

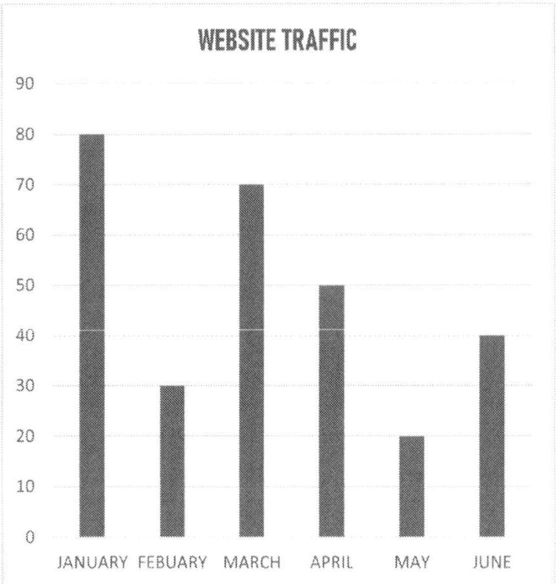

FIGURE 2.34 Ineffective title and text - the title should effectively state the values seen in the graph. X and Y axis should be easily interpreted while still being aesthetic.

Limit the Use of Uppercase Text

We live in a day and age when uppercase text can be perceived as a rude expression such as shouting. You certainly do not want your audience to feel that you are shouting data at them. Therefore, the use of uppercase text needs to be limited and carefully implemented when used. If you decide to use uppercase texts, do so in a manner that calls attention to a particular element.

Keep Chart Captions Short And Clear

Chart captions are used to summarize the data being portrayed in your charts. You need to analyze this text with an eagle eye, and any word that does not add value needs to be cut off swiftly. This means you need to chop all adjectives. Articles like *the*, *a*, and *an* should be removed where they are not required. All words that have a shorter synonym need to be replaced. Think short and crisp when you use captions.

So, what should be included in your chart captions? The first notable item is the units of measurement to represent the data in the chart. This should, of course, correspond with the data plotted in the chart. For example, you cannot have inches as the measurement in your chart and have centimeters in your caption. They need to be the same. Time periods should also be included if they are relevant to your chart. These are typically added in brackets. As for location, as a safe bet, center your caption as this generally is the most visually appealing. As a final note on this, ensure that you use sentence-style capitalization when creating captions that end those sentences with a period.

Shorten Data Labels

Labels help your audience identify the categories represented in your charts. They allow those categories to be associated with the corresponding value. These labels need to align with the categories represented in your chart. They need to be as short as possible for easy reading, especially if your chart factors in several variables. It is acceptable to use abbreviations to ensure this short length.

Suppose you find that it is not possible to shorten the length of your labels past a point where the labels do not run into each other, slant them. This diagonal view is still easily legible to most audiences. Do not rotate them as this will be hard for the audience to read.

Data Legends Must Match the Data Plotted

A legend acts as the key that clues your audience in on what you are conveying with the elements added to your charts. For example, the legend may indicate what each color in your chart represents. The first thing that you must do is ensure that the legend indeed corresponds to the data being represented. The order also needs to correspond to the order that these elements appear on the chart. For example, if red is the first color depicted on your chart, the first item in the legend needs to indicate what red represents. Lastly, the legend must be placed outside of the information plotted on the chart to ensure the chart remains uncluttered.

Titles Should Be Clear and Straightforward

Just like captions need to be kept minimally worded, so too do titles and headings. Do not confuse a title for a caption. The title of your chart needs to hold a lot less information compared to a caption. Ensure that the graph is titled in the shortest, crispest way. Those words are meant to draw the audience by capturing attention. Titles should also be void of jargon and be easy for any audience to interpret.

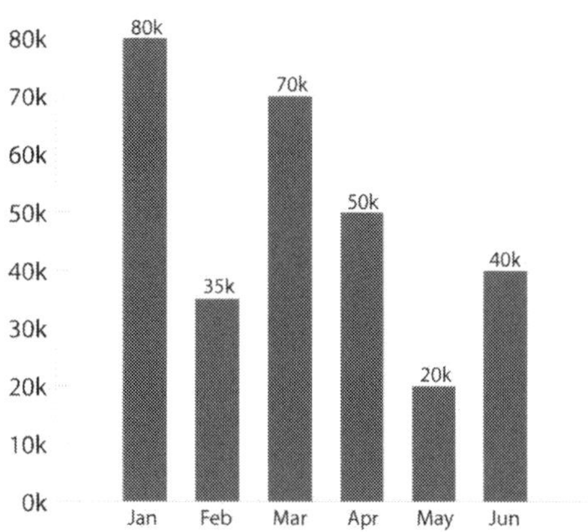

FIGURE 2.35 Proper use of text - Clear and effective title explaining what the chart is representing. Abbreviated x-axis for clean look. Additional values on top of bars can make it easy to read when specific values are required.

Just Keep It Simple

You want to wow your audience with a clear explanation of complex information. Your font is not where you want to get fancy. When in doubt, keep it simple, clear, and descriptive.

You've figured out your audience, selected the right charts, and designed them for success. Now, lets craft a winning data story.

5
CRAFTING A WINNING DATA STORY

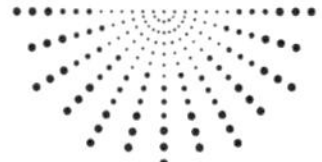

"Visualizations act as a campfire around which we gather to tell stories."

— *AL SHALLOWAY*

Movies, novels, and even data stories. They are modern examples of storytelling. However, storytelling is not new to humanity. Cave paintings show that our cavemen ancestors have been doing it a millennium back. In fact, there are cave paintings found that date back between 17,000 and 15,000 BCE.

Of course, with verbal communication came oral story storytelling, and with written language arose written storytelling. Written stories have been found dated back as far as 3,400 BCE. Those stories were written on clay tablets.

Luckily, some of the stories we find most precious are not written on such fragile things. With technological advancement, we can now listen to, read, and tell stories on radios, televisions, tablets, computers, and even on the go with our smartphones. What a way we have come!

To have withstood millennia of human changes, storytelling must be powerful indeed, and it has been shown that its powers are unlimited. Storytelling has the power to shape how we view the world and ourselves. This one thing has the ability to determine the prejudices that we develop (and yes, we all have biases) and the values and morals that we hold. It helps us understand and remember valuable information. It helps us cohabitate with each other via communication. Of course, we can deliver communication via hard facts, but stories give us context and deliver valuable insight that would have otherwise been lost.

All of these powers and more are yours to harness because by using storytelling, you can translate data into something understandable, relatable, and actionable. Through storytelling, data analysts can turn numbers that mean nothing to an audience, into a vehicle to drive change.

Just as there are steps and processes involved in creating a magnificent story through a novel or a movie, there are also steps and processes involved in creating a magnificent data story. Winging it will not do. Just as the human body is composed of specific parts to make complete anatomy, your data story needs to hold certain features for it to be complete and deliver value to your audience. Without these components, you will have a poorly executed data story.

This book was written to ensure that your data story has complete anatomy. It was written to give you the steps and processes necessary for developing a magnificent data story each and every time. This part of this book shows you how to bring all the steps and processes together beautifully.

HOW TO PRESENT YOUR DATA

It is all good and well to understand the steps and processes that go into creating a magnificent data story. However, you also need to know how to put these steps and processes together to have a well-oiled data storytelling machine. Such a machine has eight main components. These components are:

The Data Is Clearly Visible to the Audience

This component can seem obvious, but it is often the case where audiences need to squint to make out figures and texts on visualizations. What can seem clearly visible to you during the design phase of your data story can be hard to make out for your audience.

Avoid the embarrassment by getting a second opinion as to how visible the information on your charts is before you put it in front of the eyes of your audience.

The Data Illustrates the Key Points

Remember that your data means nothing to your audience until you slice it, dice it, and spice it up with the proper condiments. Then it becomes something tasty that your audience wants to digest.

Always uphold the structure of the main point of your data story, which is supported by key insights that are then further supported by points of relevant data. If your presentation does not follow that hierarchy, you need to go back to the drawing board. Anything else leaves far too much up to the interpretation of your audience. You are the one who needs to provide a clear path to solutions for your audience.

The Data Analyst Only Shares 1 Key Point from Each Chart at a Time

Each chart you develop as part of your data story has one function: to give context to a key insight. Some data analysts try to take the lazy way out and stuff several key insights into one chart. The only thing such an action will achieve is to confuse your audience.

The charts in your presentation need to be strategically aligned with the narrative you develop. The narrative needs to be paced well so that your audience does not become overwhelmed. The charts help maintain that strategic pace.

The Components of Each Chart Are Clearly Labelled

Your audience needs to gain as much information from a glance as possible without being overwhelmed. As a result, every component of your chart needs to be clearly and simply labeled. They also need to be visually impactful. Avoid that dreaded squinting effect from the audience.

Also, try to avoid abbreviations when possible in component labels as their extension might not be obvious to all audience members.

Lastly, add the component labels to each chart. Never assume that the audience will remember from viewing a previous chart.

The Data Visualizations Guide the Audience to Pre-planned 'Aha' Moments

An effective data story is a guided path to a conclusion. Think about any good tour that you have been on. There are stops along the way for you to marvel and point at before you reach that big finish. You need to provide the same experience with your data story. The conclusion is your big finish, but you also need to provide stops along the way that wow your audience. Those stops are your 'aha' moments. They are the key insights.

Make them special by verbally pointing them out as well as adding them to your charts. While you, of course, want to gently guide the audience to such moments and make the realization themselves, assume that it will fly over the heads of at least some of the audience members. Ensure that this does not happen by clearly stating these moments.

The Chart Titles Reinforce the Key Points

Another tool that leads your audience to their key insights (AKA the 'aha' moments) is the title of your charts. Just like those special stops along a guided tour spell out what the visitors will be seeing, you need to provide that part of the experience for your audience.

Ensure that the title complements the charts so that your audience is not confused. Imagine being on a tour and stopping at the "mango trees" attraction only to see apple trees. You will doubt everything else to come on that tour. The same analogy applies to titling your charts. This may seem obvious to some, but I have seen one too many titles that make little to no correlation with the data.

The Data Analyst Presents to the Audience Rather Than to the Data

Eye contact. It is a nonverbal communication method that can do a lot of things. It can intimidate. It can tell of interest without a word. It can express delight. Among the many other things it can do is that it can build a connection. Use that nonverbal communication device to your advantage when you present your data story.

Of course, there is nothing wrong with glancing at your visualizations to make references. However, far too many data analysts keep their eyes trained on the charts that they are presenting rather than their audience and miss that opportunity to form a human connection with these people. Not only that, but they also give up the chance to observe cues from the audience as to whether the audience is captivated or bored. Observing this allows the data analyst to keep on the current path or make changes on the spot to develop and maintain the connection.

HOW TO EXPLAIN YOUR CHART

As great as your visuals may be with aesthetic colors, appropriate titles and labels, and all the like, they need to be followed up with verbal communication that reinforces what is seen and adds relevant context.

I get it. Verbal presentations may not be some of our strong suits. And left to our own devices, we tend to make a muck of things. But that will not be the case. You can fall back on a methodology to make the most out of explaining your charts, and it is called Schneiderman's mantra.

Ben Schneiderman developed this mantra. Born in 1947, he is an American computer scientist and a professor at the University of Maryland. He proposed his mantra as a way for data analysts to understand how people visually engage content. An overview of this visual engagement goes like this:

1. Overview of the information
2. Zoom and filter specific parts of the information
3. Look for relevant details on demand

This mantra is used highly in interactive visualizations, but the principles are still applicable when static charts are used.

His mantra is the fifth step of developing chart presentations that wow and that are effective.

The five steps are:

1. Think about everything necessary to be included in your charts.
2. Label everything from the titles and legends to the X and Y axes.
3. Provide the context of how the data was processed to develop the charts.
4. Be intentional about the visual encoding, such as the colors and text used to develop your charts.
5. Use Schneiderman's mantra to explain the charts to the audience.

Steps 1, 2, and 4 are done before you start making your presentation. We have covered the bases as to how to do these steps. Step 3 is a matter of courtesy and allows you to avoid confusion. Simply outline your process for assimilating your data into the charts briefly in the introductory part of your presentation.

Now let's focus on step five, which outlines Schneiderman's mantra. By knowing how human beings tend to engage visual content, you can approach explaining your visualizations in a way that aligns with this natural flow. Here is a step-by-step guide to exactly how you can do this.

Provide the Overview First

You feel it when you are confronted with something visually for the first time. Your eyes move back and forth, trying to take in as much as possible in one glance. We often describe the motion as not knowing where to look first. The reason for this is because our brains are trying to decipher exactly what we are looking at. The brain has enlisted the function of the eyes to go on this fact-finding mission.

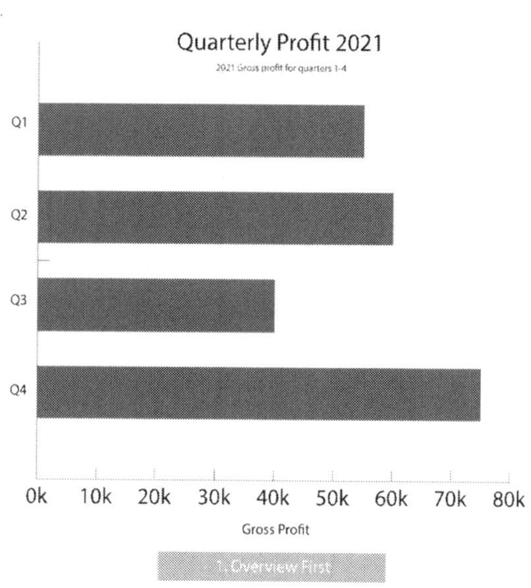

FIGURE 3 Overview of graph first - Overview of graph lets audience have a general understanding of values before making any conclusions.

Take advantage of the audience's natural inclination and aid the eyes' mission to decipher what is being visually presented to them by explaining exactly what they are looking at in the form of your visualization. This does not have to be long-winded. You only need to provide a sentence or two to describe what the chart is about. In essence, you are giving a slightly more detailed version of the title of your chart. And remember, your title is the showcase of the key insight highlighted by that chart.

Zoom and Filter

The next thing the brain is inclined to do after getting an overview of visual information is narrow in on specific things that are particularly attention-catching. It filters through all the information that is being presented and zooms in on specific details.

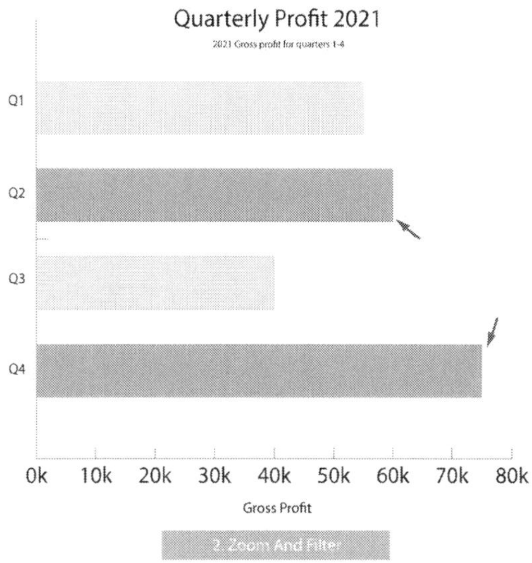

FIGURE 3.1 Zoom and filter - Highlight key points to better get your message across. Slowly lead your audience to your conclusion.

As an effective data analyst, you would have provided visual cues that are particularly attention-catching. For example, these may be the only colored bars in your bar graph or the highlighted trends in your line graph. These attention-grabbing details are what you will use to provide that 'aha' moment. Such details point your audience in a particular direction to reach the conclusion, which is the main point of your data story. Think back to our guided tour analogy, and you know what I mean. Those details support your insight (the stop before reaching the end of the tour).

This is where visual cues such as the colors you use can be of aid. For example, you may want to point out a specific line on your line chart to expand on that data. In that case, all you would have to do is say something like, "Notice this red line here..." and follow that up with your explanation.

Provide Details on Demand

Once the brain has drilled down on specific details that it finds interesting, curiosity is aroused. Therefore, it will want to know more about these particular details.

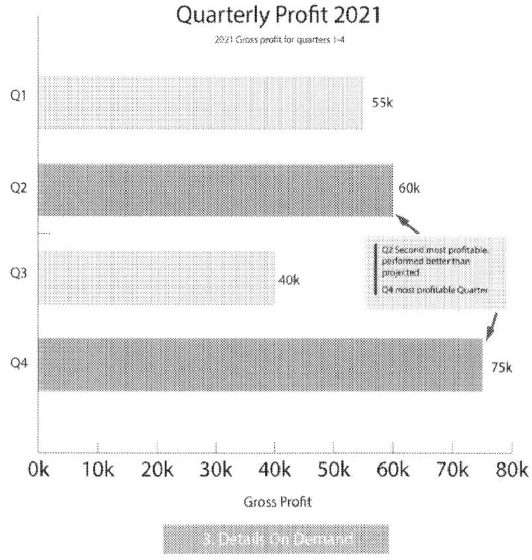

FIGURE 3.2 Details on demand - Explain key information in your chart related to specific highlighted points.

Again, this is something that you can capitalize on while delivering your data story. After you have made sure that your audience has been thoroughly captivated by the highlighted key insights, provide them with more data about them. Give them the relevant information about why this insight is relevant to the ultimate conclusion of your data story.

The best thing about using Schneiderman's mantra is that this three-step approach can be applied to explain any type of chart for any kind of situation. It is a solid approach that helps the audience understand what has been presented to them and allows data analysts to have a foolproof method of giving the audience relevant context to what is being visually presented to them. Always have this manta in the forefront of your mind when explaining your charts - overview first, zoom and filter, and finally, provide details on demand.

USING THE RIGHT VOCABULARY

From the beginning

Now that you've chosen an effective graph and designed it to work in your favour, it's time to get an idea of what vocabulary you should use when describing graphs, charts, and diagrams. Here are some phrases I like to use to catch my audience's attention right from the start.

- If you look at this graph, you will notice...
- To illustrate my point, let's look at some charts...
- Let's turn to this diagram...
- I'd like you to look at...
- If you look at this graph, you will notice...
- Let me show you this bar graph...
- Let's have a look at this pie chart...

Describing important elements

When you are describing any form of visual information, it is important to guide your audience to the key points you are trying to make. Some examples would be:

- The colored segment is for...
- The vertical axis shows...
- The shaded area describes...
- The horizontal axis represents...
- The curve here illustrates...
- The solid line shows...
- The green bar indicates....

ALWAYS HAVE SUPPORTING INFORMATION

Although a picture-perfect presentation is what we strive for, it is common to get hit with rebuttals and questions. Depending on your audience, this might be more or less prominent. Although healthy discussion is imminent and recommended, it is always good to keep some extra information on the back burner to further enhance the data's insights. Put yourself in the shoes of your audience. What areas allow for concern? What will they most likely be skeptical toward or want to know more about? It's always a good idea to have some extra insights and visualizations to fall back on, usually related to the main insights of the presentation. Supporting data is vital.

Some common questions that audiences tend to ask are:

- Is this our only course of action?
- Do you have any other figures so we can better understand the depth of your point?
- What exactly are you telling us?
- If we stay on this course, what will be the outcome?
- Do you have any concrete ideas for improvement in these areas?

Driving effective business growth is a difficult task. That's why so many businesses fail. Expect the amount of discussion to vary based on your audience and the significance of the data. A quick overview of the last quarter will be less intense than a yearly review of a failing product. Be strategic and prepare accordingly. This can make a huge impact on your presentation.

PERFORMING A GREAT EXECUTION

One of the best storytelling tactics is to give real-life examples, and I will show you what this looks like by giving you an example of what an effective data story looks like in this section. This section is a run-through of what an effective data story looks like in a real-world setting.

For such a scenario to work, you need to have gone through the steps previously outlined in this book. There is no skipping the creative process that ultimately leads you to the presentation of your charts. You would have needed to develop an engaging narrative, compile data that is relevant that aligns with that narrative and design visually appealing charts to support this relevant data. Without these supporting aspects, there is no hope of executing an excellent presentation.

With those aspects in the bag, you are prepared for the big day. You will prove your mettle as an engaging storyteller supported by data visualizations. Again, this is not something that you have to develop a new method for. There is a methodology that you can fall back on to tell great data stories.

An engaging data story has four main sections, and they are:

- The Introduction
- The rising action
- The climax
- Conclusion

How about we walk through an example and bring it all together.

. . .

LET'S say you launched a new software at the beginning of 2022, and you're analyzing the profit margins for the year (you're a software company that sells payroll software to help businesses streamline their payroll processes through automated payments and calculations). You realize that your profit margins are smaller than projected due to higher customer support and software maintenance costs than anticipated. As you acquire more customers and costs go up, it will result in smaller profit margins, and eventually losses. You need to find a possible solution to the problem and present the whole story. Let's walk through the steps to make it as straightforward as possible.

Step 1: Some questions you need to ask before you start. There are multiple options here regarding who you're presenting to and a possible solution to the problem.

The Narrative: The product/service you offer had an excellent launch and is performing well. However, the profit margins are smaller than we projected due to higher customer support and software maintenance costs. Over time you will be in the negative if action is not taken for 2023

The Players: Who exactly is in charge of making a big decision? Is it the VP of product? The Product manager? Curate your presentation to cater to this person. What do they know, what don't they know? Refer to Chapter 2 to find out who you're talking to.

For this example, we are talking to the product manager. They have some in-depth knowledge of the product and its pricing but aren't familiar with the issue you are bringing to light. We can categorize them as a "manager" and an "analytical" audience type.

The Solution: How will we solve the problem? What is the solution? It is the product manager who will make the call. But as the one analyzing the data, you have the in-depth knowledge and need to present possible solutions to the problem. How can we raise the price or add extra costs without losing customers? Can we also cut costs to enhance the profit margins?

In this case, some solutions could be:

- Raise the monthly price gradually throughout the next six months
- Increasing perceived value by marketing a new feature as an "upgrade"(then raising the price).
- Decreasing maintenance/labor costs.
- Increase the value by adding additional services/features/upgrades, then raising the price.
- Raise/Add in an additional monthly "maintenance fee" or cost for upgrades/customer support.
- Or even just raise your prices with confidence.

In this case, the best option seems to add an additional monthly "maintenance fee." While reducing costs where you can. Label this as a "Version upgrade" with a minor price increase to improve customer relations and future maintenance/updates.

Step 2: How to choose and optimize your visual strategy.

We've created a visualization representing profit and maintenance costs for 2022.

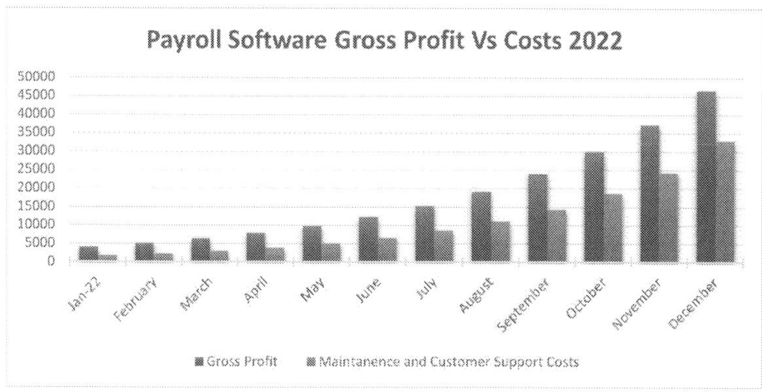

FIGURE 3.3

This is pretty standard of how most people would visualize this data. However, a line chart is a much more effective option when looking at a trajectory over time. As you can see with the 2022 numbers, profits are still fine, and although lower than expected, small tweaks should correct this. It even looks like profits could correct over time. Let's look at the same data in a line chart.

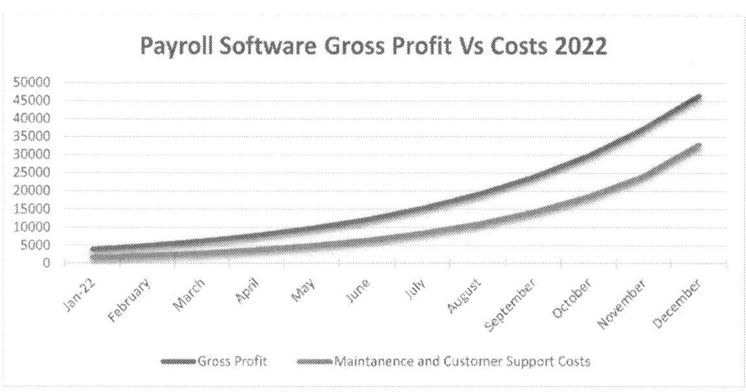

FIGURE 3.4

However, this doesn't tell the full story. After analyzing the data, we have a steady 25% growth month over month in profit. But a 30% growth month over month in costs. If you are accounting for inflation (wage increases, business cost increases, etc), Costs will be closer to 36% month over month come 2023. We can project that by April of 2023, the software will not be profitable.

Let's have a look at this in a bar chart.

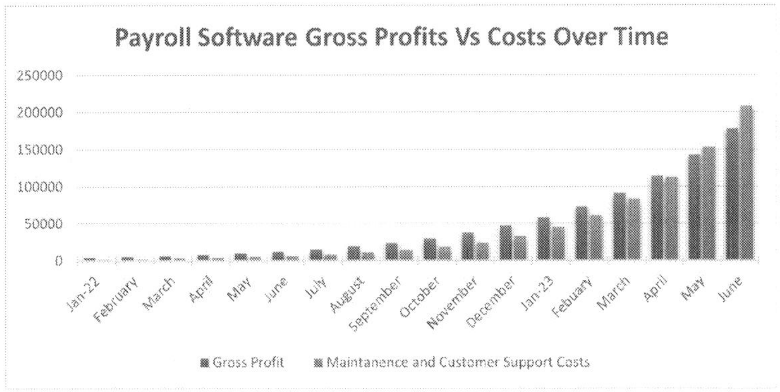

FIGURE 3.5

Some people will argue this is an effective way to visualize this data. However, it comes across as more stagnant figures than the trajectory over time. It's not easily distinguishable that the costs surpass the profits. At first glance, you might not even notice that one bar surpasses the other. It just looks like some ordinary data. Just like before, a line chart will be the most effective option.

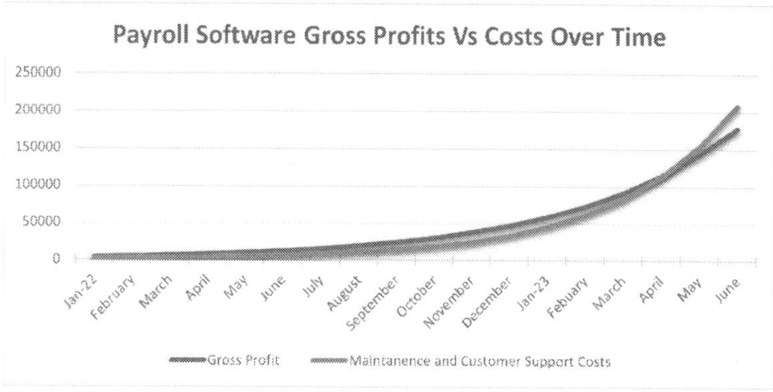

FIGURE 3.6

Now, we can easily see that as we acquire more businesses using our software, the rise in maintenance/customer support costs while considering inflation leaves us in the negative. We are rendering the software unprofitable by April of 2023. The product manager can now easily see the trajectory on their own and can visualize the detrimental outcome if action is not taken.

Step 3: Optimize your visual for maximum effectiveness

Now that we are representing our data in the most effective way possible, we must make it visually appealing to the audience. Let's revisit some essential ways to reduce clutter from chapter 4.

- Remove the chart Border.
- No Unnecessary effects (shadowing/3D, etc).
- Remove Gridlines.
- Overuse of bright/unnecessary colors.

- Shorten data labels.

This chart can be our "overview" of the initial data.

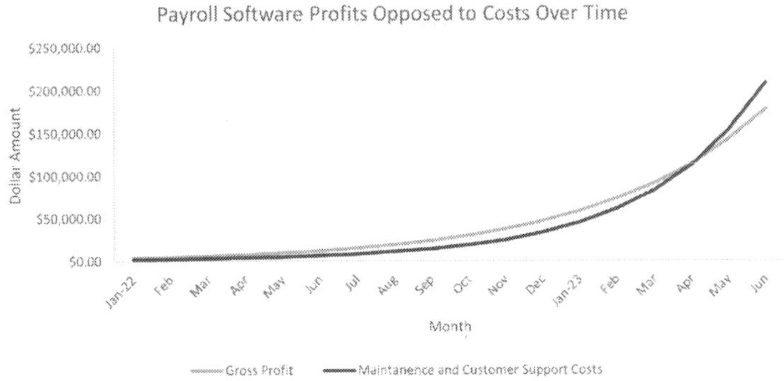

FIGURE 3.7

Now to increase the clarity of our point, let's introduce a second slide with some attentive attributes. I have labeled and highlighted the point where the maintenance/support costs outweigh the profits, Showing that we will start to make significant losses after this time frame if something isn't changed.

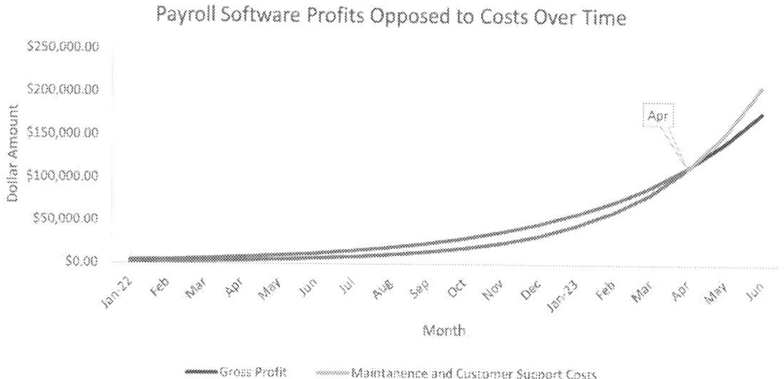

FIGURE 3.8

Step 4: Present the visual effectively.

Properly present the visual with presentation tactics used in this book, such as the sandwich approach and Schneiderman's mantra. Pair this with some specific techniques based on your audience type. You want the audience to come to a conclusion on their own. *they can see the profit margins are smaller than anticipated and will become unprofitable over time because of high maintenance/support costs. They'll need to adjust the price point or add additional maintenance fees to make up for the extra costs.*

Step 5: Present a Solution

If you did everything right, you would've known a possible solution before you even created a chart. However, if you have to relay a complicated and drastic solution, give them multiple options to consider. Explain some flaws in the other options, and then finally end up on the solution we think is the most effective and streamlined as if it is the only option. Or, potentially keep the options open and discuss the best direction. (this is only necessary with more complex problems you have to find a solution for)

In this case, the best option seems to add an additional monthly "maintenance fee." the best way to go about this is as a "Version upgrade" with a minor price increase to improve customer relations and future maintenance/updates. Show that they're receiving an upgraded and improved product overall. The original monthly subscription people pay for the software is $200. After analyzing the margins, Adding $25 per month for the subscription is enough to increase profits drastically without losing any customers. Now that we also know how high our maintenance and support costs can be with this particular software, we must do what we can to trim as much of that as possible. Suppose we can reduce costs by 10% in 2023, with the additional $25/month per customer. We are setting ourselves up for an excellent 2023. If we can make some changes at the beginning of the year, here are our projected numbers:

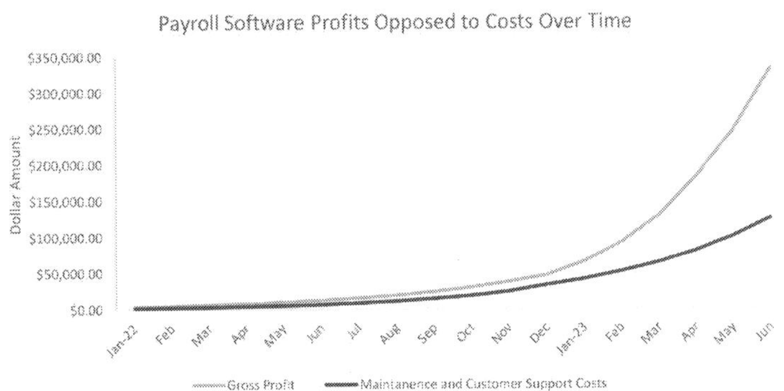

FGURE 3.9

Step 6: Bringing everything together.

Now let's bring this together as if we were presenting. By spending the extra effort doing research and creating proper charts, we can keep our presentation simple and let the charts and data speak for themselves.

Lets organize our data story like we stated before. The Introduction, The Rising Action, The Climax, The Conclusion.

THE INTRODUCTION

In a book or film, this section is a representation of the main characters going about their daily lives before they are ultimately thrown through the wringer to come out as a changed person. It is the setup to show where this character is now so that the audience has context as to how they will move through the main parts of the story. It is what allows the audience reading or watching to develop a connection with this character. When the audience cares, the introduction has performed its function and hooked these people.

In data storytelling, the introduction has the same function. It is a setup meant to give context and hook the audience. This is where the analyst will show the audience what problem brought everyone to that setting on that day, the benefits to solving that issue, and possible solutions to solving the problem. The audience needs to care about moving through the guided tour that starts with the problem and ends with the solution.

"We've analyzed the numbers for 2022, and we've noticed some issues with the long-term trajectory. As you can see, profit margins are smaller than we anticipated due to higher customer support and software maintenance costs."

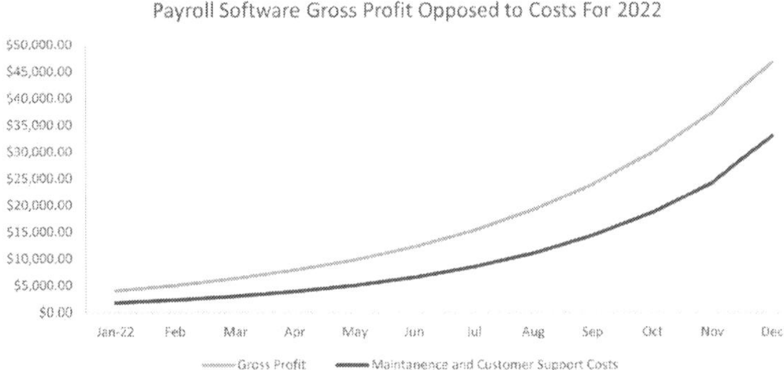

FIGURE 3.10

"Although it seems to be quite manageable, there are some more significant issues that need to be addressed with the long term trajectory.

We have set the stage by showcasing the norm and highlighting the problem that led to this data story's need. They also alluded to finding the cause of the problem and the delivery of a solution to the problem.

They have provided context and delivered the hook.

THE RISING ACTION

In books and films, this is where the main character's life changes. A catalyst causes this change and ensures no turning back from the path ahead of this person. The introduction has gotten the audience to care about this person, but this part will have the audience at the edge of their seats wanting to know what happens next.

In data storytelling, again, the analogy applies. The catalyst that incites change is the delivery of analyzed data to support the findings that highlight the problem. Many junior data analysts make a mistake here: they throw data point after data point after point at the audience. The function of this part of the story is to build anticipation of the solution to the problem. Continue to give context to the problem and support this with only relevant details. Do not be stingy but build anticipation by leaving the audience wondering where you are leading them. Keep that image of the guided tour in your mind. You do not want to see everything the tour has to offer upfront. Otherwise, what would there be for you to look forward to?

We have a steady 25% growth month over month in gross profit. But a 30% growth month over month in costs. If you are accounting for inflation (wage increases, business expenses, etc.) our costs will be closer to 36% come 2023.

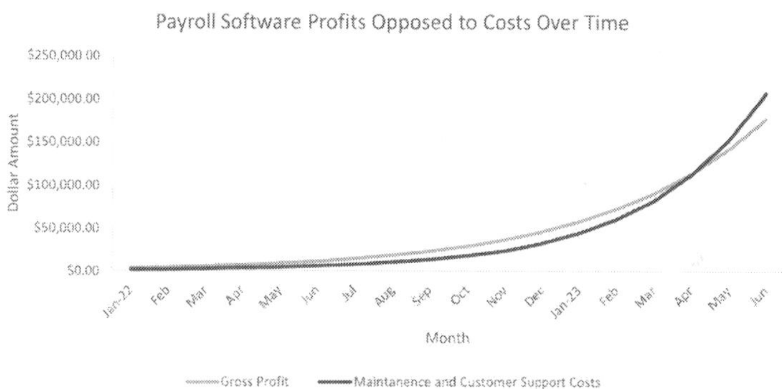

FIGURE 3.11

As can be seen, by this explanation, we are giving more context to data. At this point, they are also showcasing charts that support this context. Notice that their wording gives more details and leads the audience's focus to a particular point, which is why this problem has arisen and how it can be solved.

THE CLIMAX

This step in storytelling represents that turning point in the story where the changes that will come to fruition become clear. It is the highest point of tension in the story. It is the height of the anticipation built in the rising action step. Remember that this part will not serve its purpose unless you set the foundation with a good introduction and the anticipation developed in the rising action.

In data storytelling, the climax is your 'aha' moment. It finally reveals the things that the presenter was alluding to in the introduction and rising action portions. Things should become clear to the audience then, leaving them with a sense of fulfillment.

"As more businesses use our software, We can project that the costs will outweigh our profits by April of 2023 if no major changes are made. Rendering the software unprofitable"

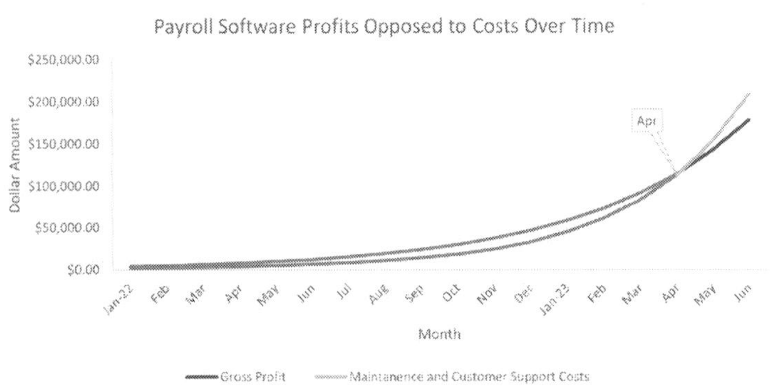

FIGURE 3.12

This speech has revealed the why of the problem that was stated from the introduction and given context in the rising action. The audience should feel relieved to know the cause of the problem and look forward to the conclusion which leads the way forward.

CONCLUSION

In a book or movie, this is the part that gives closure to the audience as it shows how the main character is settling in with the new changes. Data storytelling summarizes the entire presentation in as brief a language as possible and defines the steps that should be taken next.

The following steps can be hypothetical, a solution to how the situation can turn out if certain actions were taken or avoided, or recommendations for future action.

"After analyzing the numbers, I believe the best way to fix the trajectory is to issue a "Version upgrade" to improve customer relations and future maintenance/updates. Adding $25 per month to the subscription is more than enough to increase profits drastically without losing any customers. Now that we also know how high our maintenance and support costs can be with this particular software, it is important to do what we can to trim as much of that as possible."

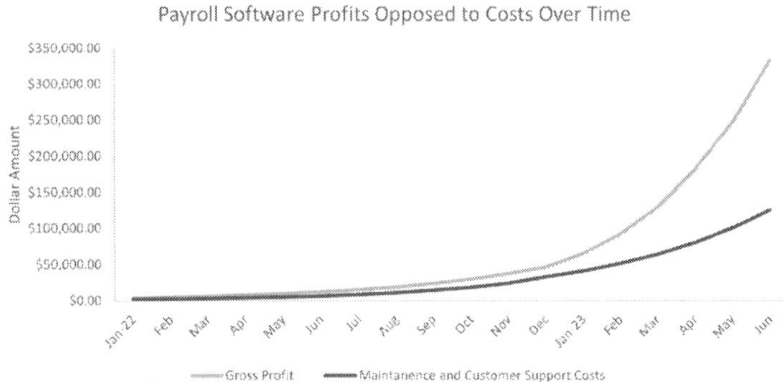

FIGURE 3.13

"As you can see, *If we can manage to reduce costs by 10%, paired with the additional \$25/month per customer. We are setting ourselves up for an excellent 2023 and beyond.*"

Overview

To create an effective data story, it starts with understanding the narrative. What do we need to present, and why? Once you figure this out, you can determine who you're presenting to and what solution you need to guide them towards. When creating visuals, we have to make sure we choose the most effective way of presenting that data to our specific audience. Is it just visually showing some values or driving conclusions in an easy to interpret manner? When you've found the best chart for the data, designing to win is a crucial step. Eliminate any unwanted clutter and make the information as clear as possible. Once your visuals are up to par, presenting the data in an effective and structured manner is the key to winning over your audience. Start with an overview of the information you've analyzed. Slowly work your way through the supporting evidence and possible solution to the problem. Ask the right questions and properly design the visuals so the audience can come to your desired conclusion with as little persuasion as possible. Let's have a look at where we started and where we ended up.

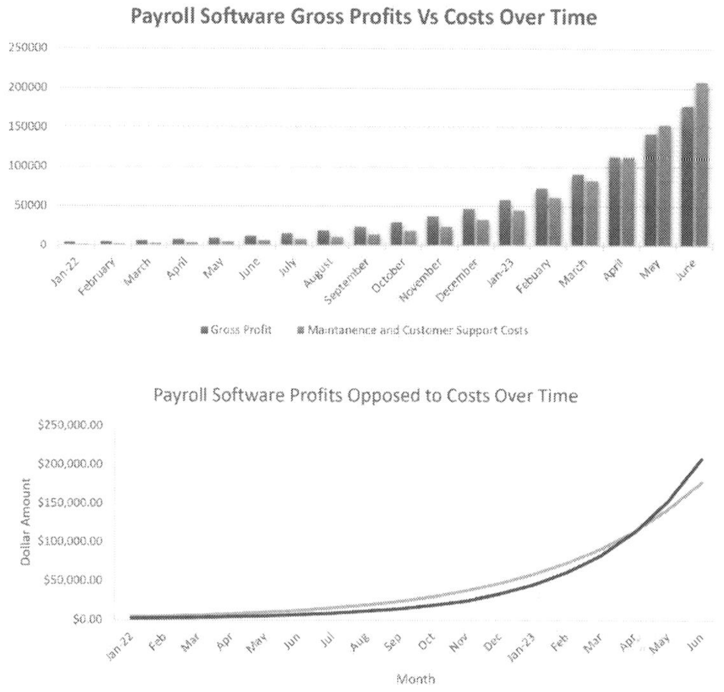

FIGURE 3.14

By utilizing the six steps above, you will be on track to create a winning data story. If you want to get some hands-on practice, try creating a scenario from a situation at work or your imagination. Create the visuals and structure them to present them to someone important.

. . .

LIKE EVERYTHING else with data storytelling, you do not have to reinvent the wheel to explain your charts right. The template has already been prepared for you. First, introduce the problem that has warranted the need for the development of this data story. Get your audience anticipating a solution by giving them context and hinting why this problem has developed with the rising action. Provide the 'aha' moment in the climax of the data story by plainly explaining the *why* that has been anticipated. And finally, leave the audience fulfilled with a conclusion that outlines possible solutions to solving this problem.

Thank you so much for making it this far!

I greatly appreciate the time you took to give my book a read. As a small indie publisher, it means a lot and I hope I am making a difference in your career.

If you have a minute or two, it would mean the world to me if you could leave a short review on Amazon. It does wonders for the book and I love hearing your thoughts! You can do so by visiting Review1.Elizabethsclarke.com, scanning the QR below, or visiting your orders page.

If you have any constructive criticism, don't hesitate to reach out to me at Contact@elizabethsclarke.com. I always look to improve my books and make necessary updates for the longevity of the content.

-Elizabeth

CONCLUSION

> "The effectiveness of data visualization can be gauged by its simplicity, relevancy, and its ability to hold the users hand during their data discover journey."
>
> — JAGAT SAIKIA

Every single day, data, so much of it, is being created. It would all look like nonsensical babble if not for people like you. Data analysts and business professionals are the translators of data, and without them, so many audiences would not know how to proceed with this data influx.

However, there is an art and a science to delivering data to an audience in an understandable, relatable, and actionable way, and that is data storytelling. You have gotten to this part of this book, and I commend you for that dedication to mastering data storytelling. You have all the tools necessary for delivering a powerful data story to your audience each and every time. From here, you can continue to expand upon your knowledge and grow your expertise to translate more complex and compelling data.

As a quick reference, here is a brief summary of what it takes to create a data story that wows and informs:

The Foundation, The Narrative

This is the narrative of your data story. The entire structure will depend on how effectively you develop the narrative. Your goals will be established here. You will also drill down on the context of your data story here. The context gives the why of this data story - why it is necessary that this data story be told. What is the problem that needs solving, and how can it be solved in actionable steps? Developing the narrative also allows you to develop an understanding of who the key players are and what information is already at their disposal. Figuring out such details will also help you to develop an introduction that hooks your audience and keeps them captivated throughout the presentation.

Captivating Your Audience

The narrative, the chart development, and all other effort and time you have put into developing a data story will be for nothing if you fail to connect with the audience you are delivering to. These people rely on you to clearly state the problem that needs to be addressed and provide possible solutions. Therefore, how to present data to them should always be at the forefront of your mind. You need to become familiar with the needs of these people, their familiarity with the subject, the best ways of communicating with them, and the best methods of influencing them in taking action after all is said and done.

Refining Your Visuals: Choosing the Right Chart

With the narrative developed and the audience figured out, you need to recreate the details in visual form. This is the function of your charts. However, not just any chart will do. You need to create naturally paced charts and designed visuals to keep your audiences informed but not overwhelmed.

This phase also means choosing the right charts to showcase data in the best light. This choice is dependent on the type of data that needs to be highlighted during your presentation. Just because some data has been put into a pie graph doesn't mean it's any more valuable than raw numbers. Make sure the chart effectively depicts the information you are presenting. The charts are intended to make the data easily understood.

Refining Your Visuals: Developing a Winning Design

Chart development is not just about having relevant data presented. Charts must also be visually appealing to your audience. This is a delicate balance that you must achieve to keep your audience engaged and interested in seeing your data story to the end. The psychology of design is something that you must fall back on to choose colors, textures, texts, and other design details that positively capture the attention of the audience and help them understand the key insights being delivered. To make your charts clean and easy to interpret, eliminate elements that don't add any informative value. Highlight key insights with attentive attributes to put your audience's attention exactly where you want it so they can quickly drive the correct conclusions on their own.

Crafting a Winning Data Story

You have all it takes to execute a winning data story once you follow the steps outlined above. These tools guide you to crafting a presentation that fulfills its purpose. The last step is execution. Luckily, Schneiderman's mantra allows you to clearly explain your charts with these steps:

1. Overview the information
2. Zoom and filter specific parts of the information
3. Look for relevant details on demand

A data story being effectively delivered has 4 main sections, and they are:

- The introduction
- The rising action
- The climax
- Conclusion

Follow that structure, and you will have this in the bag!

If there is one thing that I want you to take away after reading this book, it is that anyone can craft an engaging data story. The steps and tools have already been clearly laid out for you. This book was written in plain language to show you step by step how this methodology plays out so that you have the best chances of creating winning data stories every time. This last bit only you can perform, putting these steps and tools into good use. Don't overthink it. Just follow the methodology, expand upon it, and become an awesome data storyteller. What are you waiting for?

More Books From the Author

Scan to learn more

Scan if You're New to the World of Data

Join My Mailing List at ElizabethSClarke.com to Stay Up to Date for Future Releases and Promos!

INDEX

RESOURCES

Boyd B. (2018). The evolution of stories: from mimesis to language, from fact to fiction. *Wiley interdisciplinary reviews. Cognitive science*, 9(1), e1444. https://doi.org/10.1002/wcs.1444

Boyd, R. L., Blackburn, K. G., & Pennebaker, J. W. (2020). The narrative arc: Revealing core narrative structures through text analysis. *Science advances*, 6(32), eaba2196. https://doi.org/10.1126/sciadv.aba2196

Dettori, J. R., & Norvell, D. C. (2018). The Anatomy of Data. *Global spine journal*, 8(3), 311–313. https://doi.org/10.1177/2192568217746998

Elliot A. J. (2015). Color and psychological functioning: a review of theoretical and empirical work. *Frontiers in psychology*, 6, 368. https://doi.org/10.3389/fpsyg.2015.00368

Hattab, G., Rhyne, T. M., & Heider, D. (2020). Ten simple rules to colorize biological data visualization. *PLoS computational biology*, 16(10), e1008259. https://doi.org/10.1371/journal.pcbi.1008259

Lee, J. C., & Livesey, E. J. (2018). Rule-based generalization and peak shift in the presence of simple relational rules. *PloS one*, 13(9), e0203805. https://doi.org/10.1371/journal.pone.0203805

Li Q. (2020). Overview of Data Visualization. *Embodying Data: Chinese Aesthetics, Interactive Visualization and Gaming Technologies*, 17–47. https://doi.org/10.1007/978-981-15-5069-0_2

Marković S. (2012). Components of aesthetic experience: aesthetic fascination, aesthetic appraisal, and aesthetic emotion. *i-Perception*, 3(1), 1–17. https://doi.org/10.1068/i0450aap

Martinez-Conde, S., Alexander, R. G., Blum, D., Britton, N., Lipska, B. K., Quirk, G. J., Swiss, J. I., Willems, R. M., & Macknik, S. L. (2019). The Storytelling Brain: How Neuroscience Stories Help Bridge the Gap between Research and Society. *The Journal of neuroscience: the official journal of the Society for Neuroscience*, 39(42), 8285–8290. https://doi.org/10.1523/JNEUROSCI.1180-19.2019

Mastandrea, S., Fagioli, S., & Biasi, V. (2019). Art and Psychological Well-Being: Linking the Brain to the Aesthetic Emotion. *Frontiers in psychology*, 10, 739. https://doi.org/10.3389/fpsyg.2019.00739

Midway S. R. (2020). Principles of Effective Data Visualization. *Patterns (New York, N.Y.)*, 1(9), 100141. https://doi.org/10.1016/j.patter.2020.100141

Plante, T. B., & Cushman, M. (2020). Choosing color palettes for scientific figures. *Research and practice in thrombosis and hemostasis*, 4(2), 176–180. https://doi.org/10.1002/rth2.12308

Ranganathan, P., & Gogtay, N. J. (2019). An Introduction to Statistics - Data Types, Distributions, and Summarizing Data. *Indian journal of critical care medicine: peer-reviewed, official publication of Indian Society of Critical Care*

Medicine, 23(Suppl 2), S169–S170. https://doi.org/10.5005/jp-journals-10071-23198

Suzuki, W. A., Feliú-Mójer, M. I., Hasson, U., Yehuda, R., & Zarate, J. M. (2018). Dialogues: The Science and Power of Storytelling. *The Journal of neuroscience: the official journal of the Society for Neuroscience*, 38(44), 9468–9470. https://doi.org/10.1523/JNEUROSCI.1942-18.2018

Wolfe, J. M., & Utochkin, I. S. (2019). What is a preattentive feature?. *Current opinion in psychology*, 29, 19–26. https://doi.org/10.1016/j.copsyc.2018.11.005

L.C.T. (2020, July 7). *How to Tell a Story With Data*. Lucidchart. Retrieved November 2, 2021, from https://www.lucidchart.com/blog/how-to-tell-a-story-with-data

Goldmeier, J. M. (2019, November 12). *The only data visualization guide you'll ever need (in 5 principles)*. LinkedIn. Retrieved November 2, 2021, from https://www.linkedin.com/pulse/only-data-visualization-guide-youll-ever-need-5-jordan-goldmeier

Goldmeier, J. M. (2019, November 12). *The only data visualization guide you'll ever need (in 5 principles)*. LinkedIn. Retrieved November 2, 2021, from https://www.linkedin.com/pulse/only-data-visualization-guide-youll-ever-need-5-jordan-goldmeier

Infogram. (n.d.). *How to Choose the Right Chart for Your Data*. https://infogram.com/page/choose-the-right-chart-data-visualization

Gulbis, J. B. (n.d.). *Data Visualization – How to Pick the Right Chart Type?* EazyBI. Retrieved November 2, 2021, from https://eazybi.com/blog/data-visualization-and-chart-types

Yi, M. (2019, August 23). *A Complete Guide to Bar Charts*. Chartio. Retrieved November 2, 2021, from https://chartio.com/learn/charts/bar-chart-complete-guide/

Yi, M. (2019b, September 24). *A Complete Guide to Stacked Bar Charts*. Chartio. Retrieved November 2, 2021, from https://chartio.com/learn/charts/stacked-bar-chart-complete-guide/

Yi, M. (2019b, August 29). *A Complete Guide to Pie Charts*. Chartio. Retrieved November 2, 2021, from https://chartio.com/learn/charts/pie-chart-complete-guide/

Marr, B. (2021, July 13). *Why You Shouldn't Use Pie Charts In Your Dashboards And Performance Reports*. Bernard Marr. Retrieved November 2, 2021, from https://bernardmarr.com/why-you-shouldnt-use-pie-charts-in-your-dashboards-and-performance-reports/?contentID=1779#:%7E:text=From%20a%20design%20point%20of,data%20more%20complicated%20than%20before.

Yi, M. (2019c, September 13). *A Complete Guide to Line Charts*. Chartio. Retrieved November 2, 2021, from https://chartio.com/learn/charts/line-chart-complete-guide/

Yi, M. (2019d, September 16). *A Complete Guide to Area Charts*. Chartio. Retrieved November 2, 2021, from https://chartio.com/learn/charts/area-chart-complete-guide/#:%7E:text=An%20area%20chart%20combines%20the,like%20in%20a%20bar%20chart.

R. (2020b, March 8). *Presenting data visualization to engage your audience*. Medium. Retrieved November 2, 2021, from https://uxdesign.cc/presenting-data-visualization-to-engage-your-audience-815eb6a43a62

Yi, M. (2019f, October 16). *A Complete Guide to Scatter Plots*. Chartio. Retrieved November 2, 2021, from https://chartio.com/learn/charts/what-is-a-scatter-plot/

Brown, L. (n.d.). *Wondershare Fotophire Online Support Center*. Wondershare. Retrieved November 2, 2021, from https://photo.wondershare.com/graph-maker/best-graphing-software.html

Verma, R. (2021, February 26). *Data Visualization: Top 5 Most Important Things to Know*. Loginworks. Retrieved November 2, 2021, from https://www.loginworks.com/blogs/data-visualization-top-5-most-important-things/

V. (2019, February 13). *Preattentive Attributes in Visualization - An Example*. Daydreaming Numbers. Retrieved November 2, 2021, from http://daydreamingnumbers.com/blog/preattentive-attributes-example/

Preattentive Visual Properties and How to Use Them in Information Visualization. (2018, October 2). The Interaction Design Foundation. Retrieved November 2, 2021, from https://www.interaction-design.org/literature/article/preattentive-visual-properties-and-how-to-use-them-in-information-visualization

Horne, J. (2020, June 5). *Neuroaesthetics and Informative Art | iDashboards Blog*. IDashboards |. Retrieved November 2, 2021, from https://www.idashboards.com/blog/2017/08/23/neuroaesthetics-and-informative-art/

Baltusevičius, G. (2021, February 2). *How to Do Storytelling with Data Using Visualizations*. Blog | Whatagraph. Retrieved

November 2, 2021, from https://whatagraph.com/blog/articles/data-using-visualizations

Bowers, M. (2020, October 20). *Numbers Shouldn't Lie – An Overview of Common Data Visualization Mistakes*. Toptal Design Blog. Retrieved November 2, 2021, from https://www.toptal.com/designers/ux/data-visualization-mistakes

I. (2018, November 29). *Dos and Don'ts: Data Visualization Tips Before and After*. Medium. Retrieved November 2, 2021, from https://medium.com/@Infogram/dos-and-donts-data-visualization-tips-before-and-after-f1d65a7b6402

M. (2021, June 17). *7 Best Practices for Using Color in Data Visualizations*. Sigma Computing. Retrieved November 2, 2021, from https://www.sigmacomputing.com/blog/7-best-practices-for-using-color-in-data-visualizations/#:%7E:text=Why%20color%20use%20in%20data%20visualization%20matters&text=Using%20color%20strategically%20helps%20viewers,visualization%20is%20trying%20to%20tell.

Makulec, A. (n.d.). *Identifying Your Audience*. Slideshare. Retrieved November 2, 2021, from https://www.slideshare.net/AmandaMakulec/identifying-your-audience-40086476

Sleeper, R. (2021, January 2). *Vital Question 1: Who is the Audience?* Playfair Data. Retrieved November 2, 2021, from https://playfairdata.com/vital-question-1-who-is-the-audience/

S. (2018b, May 25). *Presenting complex data? Engage your audience with these 10 tips*. Medium. Retrieved November 2, 2021, from https://speakerhubhq.medium.com/presenting-complex-data-engage-your-audience-with-these-10-tips-232509301a4d

Made in the USA
Middletown, DE
06 November 2022

14302971R00113